TEST YOUR OWN APTITUDE

3RD EDITION

Jim Barrett • Geoff Williams

KOGAN
PAGE

First published in Great Britain in 1980

Second edition 1990
Third edition 2003

Kogan Page Limited
120 Pentonville Road
London N1 9JN
United Kingdom
www.kogan-page.co.uk

British Library Cataloguing-in-Publication Data

A CIP record for this book is available from the British Library.

ISBN 0 7494 3887 8

Typeset by Saxon Graphics Ltd, Derby
Printed and bound in Great Britain by Clays Ltd, St Ives plc

Contents

Preface to the third edition

Why change a good thing? The only satisfactory reason is to make it even better. *Test Your Own Aptitude* has been demonstrably 'good'. It has been a 'bestseller' in Great Britain and has been adopted as a standard text by official careers services. Having been translated into numerous languages, it has assisted thousands of people globally to discover their potential. Yet the world of work has changed. Many of the popular careers of a decade ago are now barely to be found, while new ones have appeared. This latest edition brings the process of matching talent to opportunity up to date.

Although job titles and job content may have altered, the intellectual processes that we use are the same. So, what is new is applying the same raw, human talents to types of work unknown to previous generations. There are two major reasons for this. Firstly, new work activities have arisen largely as a result of the advent of new technologies. Secondly, the perception of what is a 'career' has changed, becoming increasingly defined by an individual rather than an establishment. This is more risky because there is less security of tenure in many careers and a less well defined 'career path'. But it also offers greater scope for variety and change. The 'job for life' is being replaced by the concept of 'self-managed career'.

One thing is for sure, your own responsibility for your enjoyment and success is even more up to you! Our concept of matching potential to a career is even more relevant today than it was when this book was first published. And, even though we predicted the increase in the use of tests for vocational choice and job selection, the degree to which we have been proved right is quite astonishing – the use of tests within organizations has become commonplace. Therefore this book continues to employ the same well proven method of finding out what you can do, your hidden strengths and what is going to motivate you.

Most of the tests and questionnaires found in the previous edition have required only prudent modernizing. The addition of extra tests and an expanded index of careers ensure that you have all you require to test yourself and that you have sufficient information to make informed choices in relation to the opportunities offered in the 21st century.

Who am I? – Understanding myself better

This book is designed as a self-help guide for everyone who wants a successful career. It is founded on solid scientific research and good psychological practice, but it is also a book which is intended to give you some fun. Combining a serious objective with having fun is part of our whole approach. In the same way, there is no reason why your career should not be fun; in fact, there is plenty of evidence to suggest that if you do have fun at work you are probably more productive as well. So if you are down in the dumps about your career – either because you do not know what to do or because you are bored – read on. We believe that what you do is largely up to you. If you are not happy with your present situation, change it. This book intends to help you to do whatever you want with your career.

This book is aimed principally at two groups of people: those who have not yet started on a career and those who have had at least one job but still do not feel that they are in the career which really suits them. But it could be that you belong to a third group who just enjoy a book like this – perhaps you combine pleasure with just 'checking up on yourself'.

Whatever your reasons for reading the book, it can help you to make better decisions about what you should do in the future. It is a sad fact that most people stumble into jobs – sad because unless people find a job that suits them they will never have the opportunity to use their potential. It is also a waste of human resources and a likely cause of frustration and stress at a personal level. There is all too often an unplanned move from school to college and then on to a professional qualification. Sometimes people go straight from school to jobs in the vicinity, no matter how unique their individual potential or how restricted the range of local opportunities. People often go for the job that seems to offer them the most money or the greatest security in the short term, and are completely unaware of how their own psychology might be at odds with the job in the longer term. Other people 'follow in father's footsteps'; or maybe they abide by what parents, school or friends expect.

When you come to choose a career you should be aware of two things: first, you should know yourself and second, you should know what the world offers. In the end, your own success and happiness – however you measure these things – are determined by you. What makes somebody else content in a career will not necessarily apply to you. This is the time for you to make decisions on your own personal choices by establishing what you can do best and what you want to do most.

This book will help you to structure your career planning. 'Structure' is the key word and, if you follow the approach outlined here, you will make better informed and ultimately more creative career choices. You should work through and apply the three structured models of career/potential matching and give yourself a framework which will allow you to clarify (or sensibly scotch) your plans for developing yourself in your career. When you have worked through the various exercises which form the bulk of the book you can eventually put it all together in Chapter 5, Who I will become – Applying my potential.

The tests and questionnaires (often referred to as 'psychometrics' because their purpose is to measure mental processes) will give you an idea of what you can naturally do best (abilities), what suits your style and behaviour (personality), and what is likely to stimulate your interests and attitudes (motivation). The relevance of this basic information to your occupational decisions is then explained. More than quickly pinpointing the ideal career for you, this information is intended to provide a structured system for your own critical self-assessment. This will be of continuing service to you because the natural potential the tests elicit does not change much over time. The results will also be relevant even though changing technology may alter some career prospects.

Abilities

What we are seeking to establish is the real you. This is the person you want to be and not necessarily the person you are now. It is what you could become if you 'self-actualized'. This is why we often use the word 'ability' which has a special meaning in psychology, referring to your natural potential as well as what you can do after training. Ability is a reservoir of potential. Maybe your experience to date has not given your true ability a chance to come through.

The ability tests seek to identify those talents which are not solely dependent on learning and knowledge. In testing your underlying ability you may well discover some aptitude which you have not exploited and which could be developed.

It is not always easy for a lay person to understand how ability tests reveal anything about performance in the real world. What the tests do is to sample certain ways of comprehension, reasoning and problem solving. The tests themselves will seem removed from the ordinary daily routine but, in fact, they sample the same potential which is needed in the real world. It is probably self-evident that all human endeavour, whether it be building bridges, voyaging in space or creating poetry, is an expression of electrical and chemical connections which take place in a person's mind!

As the ability tests minimize the emphasis which is so often placed upon education and qualifications, deductions can be made, such as: 'This person has a level of reasoning ability which is higher than the average for science undergraduates'. Given information of the kind, it is fair to predict that the person in question could take a science degree, provided that other factors such as educational opportunities were present. Also important when taking a science degree is of course the element of motivation. However, if our potential seems greater for arts subjects than for science it seems practical to stop wasting time doing something which is going to give us a mediocre result when developing our stronger potential could bring us greater success.

Tests are extremely useful in revealing what a person can do. They are not so good at showing what a person cannot do – simply because determination really can move mountains. It is enough to say that over the years tests have proved excellent predictors of an individual's performance and the type of work at which he or she is likely to excel. This is a significant advance on the old IQ test which simply gave a figure that did not mean a great deal by itself. Thus, the fact that you and I both have IQ scores of 100 (average) does not really help us very much because your 100 will be completely different from mine. You may get a 100 because you are good at arithmetic while I may get a 100 because I am good at seeing how mechanical things work. It is our differences which describe us, not our similarities, and it is our differences that we must observe if we are going to locate these properly in the jigsaw puzzle which is the world of work.

The structured model we use provides you with basic information on all the major areas of underlying potential. Your relative strength in these tests can reveal an enormous amount relating to the type of education, training and work in which you are going to perform most quickly and successfully. It follows as well that you are likely to be happiest doing what you have the potential to do best. Perhaps the major cause of discontent at work is when people feel they have abilities which cannot be used in what they are doing.

Personality

In most occupations abilities can only be used effectively if certain dispositional and behavioural characteristics also exist. The mathematician needs discipline as well as intelligence; a social worker needs to be a logical thinker but selflessness, consideration and patience are more important; the business manager may need to be numerate but also needs to be assertive as well as empathetic. The personality and motivation chapters (Chapters 3 and 4) must therefore be treated as seriously as the abilities chapter (Chapter 2).

Human beings are extremely flexible in terms of the conditions as well as the relationships they are prepared to tolerate. Sometimes they will deceive themselves as much as they deceive others by pretending that they are putting up with something because they really want to. People often toil for years in situations which do not suit their personalities. In circumstances of slavery or serfdom, personality was irrelevant. But this is not the case in today's world and organizations of all kinds, both in the public and private sectors, are increasingly taking the personality of employees into account.

It is now well known that the productive output of an organization is influenced by the extent to which a personality is suited to the work in hand. When this is not the case, there tends to be internal friction between employees, with a consequent loss of output. It does not matter whether by 'productive' we mean the quantity of what is actually produced or the work atmosphere: bad quality atmosphere leads to bad quality product, whereas output and quality go up when people are happy. How to create the most efficient, happy organization is described by Jim Barrett in *Total Leadership*, published by Kogan Page.

Personality is therefore important, even though this may not be apparent in the short term since most of us can tolerate stresses and strains for a while. It is in the long term and for our own well-being that we need work which is suited to our personality.

It is sometimes thought that personality changes and that we could therefore all adapt ourselves to any kind of work. But the idea that the situation creates the person is largely erroneous because over time people will tend to gravitate to work which suits them. The fact that our personality remains constant is shown in the fact that we know each other and know what to expect of each other. Our personality is as enduring as our physical characteristics. Although the most dramatic changes of personality take place as we mature into adulthood, there are still parts of ourselves that remain constant, even from childhood. We do change, but the changes brought about as the result of experience usually take place very slowly. All who read this book will have constant personality elements with which they and others are familiar and which will continue to define their potential for some time.

Tests of personality usually take the form of questions about private thoughts, feelings and ways of behaving. This is where you have to be honest if you want a realistic appraisal of your capabilities. Personality tests are different from ability tests because there are no right or wrong answers. What emerges is simply right for you because it is the real you. Although you might wish you were endowed with characteristics you do not have, perhaps because you admire those characteristics in others, it may be helpful to remind yourself that those people may see something which they admire in you. For example, people frequently say that they wish they were more extroverted, because they want to be more sociable at parties, able to stand up and make a speech, popular and the centre of attention. Ironically, we have found that the extrovert often admires people with a reflective and perhaps more studious temperament, feeling that introverts achieve more in meaningful ways. There really is no such thing as being 'better than' as far as personality is concerned; it is simply an issue of what is appropriate!

As with the structure of the ability model, the personality model provides a descriptive framework of personality which gives you practical 'plugs' for relating your temperament to different careers in a systematic and objective process.

Motivation

If you ask people what they are really interested in doing they may feel that they know the answer. These are among the lucky few! Most people are unsure and usually it is either because they do not know their own potential or because they do not know what opportunities exist for them. Some people have 'pie in the sky' ideas, in which they feel they might be miraculously transported to a situation where they are famous or rich or leading a more exciting life. In the real world it does not happen like this.

The motivational tests are helpful in showing you where you may be getting your ambitions completely wrong. The structured model we use looks beneath your temporary interests and beyond your (perhaps) limited knowledge of careers because it allows you to express some measure of your underlying aspirations against the whole range of possibilities.

Whether you are still young and have yet to start out on a career or whether you are now rethinking your career, your underlying interests will have some firmness and remain constant over time. It is true that, as with personality, a person's interests change as they mature. In the early part of your life your interests may have been dictated by access to particular experiences or kinds of information or be encouragement from parents or close friends. Without some form of proper comparison – which is what the motivational model provides – many of us think that, given the opportunity, we could perform just as well as a famous singer, make better decisions than certain politicians, write books, grow flowers, make discoveries, help others or perhaps get away from it all – the possibilities are endless. The key thing is to establish what you are really interested in, then you are likely to do it well and experience satisfaction. People are sometimes uncertain how strong their interests really are; our structured, objective system will help you to consider lots of possibilities and then show you how strongly you feel about one type of career or another.

You will find that the tests of motivation are often deceptively simple, such as asking you to choose the job which you prefer out of a pair. You will also be asked what sort of activities appeal to you and perhaps this will stop you from saying at the outset, 'Oh, I couldn't do that' or 'I'd never get the qualifications for that', which may not, in the end, be fair comments to make about yourself. If we establish what appeals to you first of all without imposing limitations, the other structured results of personality and ability can help to determine how far and in what manner you should travel down one career route as opposed to another.

Getting what I want from work

There may be numerous factors which could be important for special forms of work or even in particular situations at work but the structured approach given in this book will be sufficient in providing an overall guide. Otherwise there are general considerations which need to be taken into account before you make any firm decisions about what you are going to do.

First, you will have to bear in mind that some careers demand physical characteristics which you do not have. Second, you might find a career which is ideal for you, but have to face the fact that it is impossible to obtain the qualification required because the educational system will not permit entry at your age. The circumstances in which you find yourself are likely to be the most important factor. By circumstances we mean where you live, your family ties, and so on, all of which must be borne in mind. For example, there may be many factors to prevent a person from dropping everything and setting off to pursue a lifelong ambition. It is not to say that circumstances are always negative or will always tie you down – it is sometimes a matter of sorting out what is going to be most important to you at any given time. However, it stands to reason that it may not be possible to achieve one thing at the expense of another.

Those people who are rethinking their careers will experience more difficulty than those just starting out because their circumstances are likely to be more complicated. People in mid-career frequently encounter a risk factor associated with giving up a job and the consequent stresses on a dependent family as well as other social and economic difficulties. Many people feel that relative discontent with some aspects of work is a small price to pay for family security and happiness. It is sometimes a question of making a compromise but compromising with full awareness is often better then simply 'putting up with' a situation because you feel there is no choice. In fact, there is always a choice and the assessment of yourself should ultimately consist of sorting out the relative importance of your present circumstances in line with the information derived from the structured analysis of yourself.

We believe that the information you will gain about yourself from working through this book will be beneficial. It is better to have information than not to have it; and you are not obliged to do anything with it.

When faced with test and questionnaire results, it is sensible to ask whether the results seem logical and 'fit' you well, however surprising they may be. This does not imply that the tests will tell you what you know already. Instead, they will tend to make more explicit ideas, assumptions, feelings and capabilities which you may long have been aware of, but which you have been keeping at the back of your mind or perhaps even hiding from yourself.

To sum up, the approach used in this book can give you valuable insight into ways in which your potential may be used more effectively. It can be an extremely useful objective check for those in mid-career; it can be useful for young people requiring guidance on the kind of education which would suit them best and on the type of career in which they would be most successful; it can also be valuable for people considering second careers. As we have already said, although it is a serious book, you can have fun with it and our intention is that, whoever you are and whatever you want, the outcome will be positive for you.

What can I do? – My abilities

Our abilities are a mixture of our underlying natural ability and our experience and attainment.

You already know a great deal about your attainment, that is, the kind of qualifications you already possess and the experience that you gained in acquiring them. From this you know what kind of activities you find easiest and which you find most difficult.

Unfortunately, however, many people do not always choose the right subjects at school, the right subjects being those which we can study most easily. All too frequently our choices are determined by other considerations such as how much we like and respect various teachers, how good they are as teachers, what subjects our parents and friends think are most 'suitable' and, of course, what options are offered by the school. Once we have started to specialize it becomes increasingly difficult to have a clear idea of what else might be available.

In this book we are more concerned with our underlying abilities, that is, the way we naturally approach problems and difficulties and our innate methods of reasoning. Some of these abilities relate quite well to academic subjects while others do not. Thus, although we may find that our abilities match the subjects we have enjoyed and completed, we may also find some 'hidden' talents which we have not yet fully explored.

Most of us can do most subjects to a greater or lesser extent. The major differences are shown by the ease with which we can cope with new problems in a particular area. Also, we can often disguise weakness in an ability if we have considerable determination and perseverance.

We are likely to be more productive, however, if we are using our best abilities to their fullest extent rather than relying on those which are not so strong. These are best left as supporters. In this way we use the minimum energy to gain the maximum benefit. In career terms this means that we are likely to move faster and further than if we are constantly having to struggle to keep up.

The ability tests

In this chapter you are presented with a series of tests. They are all different and it is important that you ignore any thoughts that you will not be any good at a test even before you start. Such thoughts may prevent you giving your true performance. It is important that you do not give up or avoid one of the tests, so try hard on each of them.

Each test has a strict time limit, but they are purposely designed so that you cannot finish all of the items in the time given. This will give you an idea of how powerful you are when having to reason in this area. If you had unlimited time you could probably complete most of the questions accurately but this would give very little idea of which way of reasoning was the most suitable and easiest for YOU. Therefore, be strict with yourself about the time limits. You will need a timer so that you can be accurate about this – a countdown timer is best.

Try to approach the tests as though you really were sitting them under examination conditions. Make sure you are fully prepared before you start the test, doing everything fairly so that you get a result that really does reflect your abilities.

Make sure you have spare paper for rough working and pens or pencils with you before you start each test. Do not mark this book if it is not your own; all your answers can be written down on spare paper if necessary.

Do not guess the answers to any of the tests. If you are almost certain, but cannot be absolutely sure your answer is correct, it is probably best to take a chance and mark the answer you think is best. However, too much guessing will count against you, as you will discover when you come to mark your answers.

Read the instructions carefully and do the practice examples, making sure you fully understand what the test involves before you start. As with all the tests and questionnaires in this book, it is possible to make the results different from what is accurate but you will get most value from them if you take them seriously.

Verbal reasoning

This test is to see how you reason with words.

For each question there are four alternative answers. Circle or underline the one which you think is correct. There are different types of question and here are a few to try.

The first one has been done for you to show you how to mark the answer.

Sample questions

1. Boy is to Man as Girl is to
   (a) Elephant   (b) Children   (c) <u>Woman</u>   (d) Horse

2. Rock is closest in meaning to
   (a) Stone   (b) Mountain   (c) Roll   (d) Water

3. Cook is to Kitchen as Mechanic is to
   (a) Machine   (b) Workshop   (c) Oil   (d) Make

4. North is the opposite of
   (a) South   (b) East   (c) Compass   (d) Hot

5. What is closest in meaning to Passageway?
    (a) Passport   (b) Step   (c) Ticket   (d) Corridor

Answers and explanation

1. (c) The question is about 'humans' so 'elephant' and 'horse' would not be correct. 'Children' is wrong because 'girl' would not become 'children' in the same way that 'boy' becomes a 'man'. 'Boy' becomes a 'man' and 'girl' becomes a 'woman' has the same relationship and makes the best sense.

2. (a) 'Stone' is the best answer, although none of the alternatives can be said to be exactly the same as rock. 'Mountain' is a possibility, but is not as adequate as 'stone', which is closer to the scale and substance of 'rock'.

3. (b) The best relationship is the place where a person works.

4. (a) 'East' is at right angles to 'north'. 'Compass' has an association with 'north', which is a point on the compass, but is not the opposite. 'Hot' has no relationship at all. 'South' is exactly the opposite of 'North'.

5. (d) 'Passport', 'step' and 'ticket' are all to do with moving or travel, but 'corridor' has a close relationship with 'passageway', which is a route of access.

Now you can start the full test which begins on the next page. You have *10 minutes* to do as much as you can. You must work as accurately as you can and as fast as you can. When you are ready, start the clock and begin.

Testing verbal reasoning

1. Ocean is to Pond as Deep is to
   (a) Shallow   (b) Well   (c) Sea   (d) Lake

2. Early is the opposite of
   (a) Evening   (b) Late   (c) Postpone   (d) Breakfast

3. Man is to Masculine as Woman is to
   (a) Intuitive   (b) Madam   (c) Girl   (d) Feminine

4. What does Frozen mean?
   (a) Glued   (b) Liquid   (c) Solid   (d) Water

5. Circle is to Sphere as Square is to
   (a) Ball   (b) Cube   (c) Polygon   (d) Triangle

6. Army is to Land as Navy is to
   (a) Sea   (b) Mountains   (c) Ships   (d) RAF

7. What means the same as Portion?
   (a) Whole   (b) Part   (c) Chip   (d) None

8. Sock is to Foot as Hat is to
   (a) Band   (b) Hair   (c) Head   (d) Face

9. What does Solitary mean?
   (a) Crowd   (b) Diamond   (c) Partner   (d) Alone

10. Wise is to Foolish as Vain is to
    (a) Modest   (b) Pretty   (c) Conceit   (d) Proud

11. Dynamic is the opposite of
    (a) Electrical   (b) Tardy   (c) Static   (d) Resistant

12. Horse is to Jockey as Car is to
    (a) Vehicle   (b) Passenger   (c) Taxi   (d) Chauffeur

13. Acquiesce is the opposite of
    (a) Clumsy   (b) Obstacle   (c) Quit   (d) Protest

14. What does Debate mean?
    (a) Comment   (b) Talk   (c) Argue   (d) Create

15. Which would be third in alphabetical order?
    (a) Sevene   (b) Severn   (c) Seveen   (d) Seven

16. Sentence is to Paragraph as Word is to
    (a) Letter   (b) Sentence   (c) Paragraph   (d) Phrase

17. Which is the odd one out?
    (a) Speech   (b) Peroration   (c) Aside   (d) Saunter

18. Eagle is to Eyrie as Fox is to
    (a) Lair   (b) Cave   (c) Web   (d) Hole

19. Which is the odd one out?
    (a) Seminal   (b) Germane   (c) Propagative   (d) Derivative

20. Which is the penultimate letter of the word REST?
    (a) R   (b) E   (c) S   (d) T

21. What is a Turbine?
    (a) Fish   (b) Engine   (c) Tower   (d) String

22. Capital is to Interest as Labour is to
    (a) Conservative   (b) Wages   (c) Authority   (d) Machinery

23. Never is to Seldom as Always is to
    (a) Occasional   (b) Usual   (c) Often   (d) Every time

24. Certainty is the opposite of
    (a) Correctness   (b) Precision   (c) Dubiety   (d) Infinite

25. Which is the odd one out?
    (a) Terse   (b) Compact   (c) Angry   (d) Curt

26. Bolt is to Nut as Hook is to
    (a) Screw   (b) Eye   (c) Door   (d) Grass

27. Which is the odd one out?
    (a) Lock   (b) Quay   (c) Bollard   (d) Anchor

28. Heredity is to Environment as Nature is to
    (a) Nurture   (b) Ancestry   (c) Health   (d) Animal

29. What is an Edifice?
    (a) Building   (b) Illness   (c) Boatyard   (d) Executive

30. Scabbard is to Sword as Arrow is to
    (a) Tourniquet   (b) Sheath   (c) String   (d) Quiver

31. Feather is to Bird as Fence is to
    (a) Farm   (b) Stake   (c) Hedge   (d) Warehouse

32. Irascible is the opposite of
    (a) Striking   (b) Flamboyant   (c) Irritable   (d) Phlegmatic

33. Nurse is to Doctor as Secretary is to
    (a) Dentist   (b) Typewriter   (c) Executive   (d) Desk

34. Which is the odd one out?
    (a) Marriage   (b) Annul   (c) Divorce   (d) Separation

35. Which is the odd one out?
    (a) Dog   (b) Hunt   (c) Fox   (d) Stalk

36. Colour is to Bleach as Flushed is to
    (a) Blush   (b) Roseate   (c) Watered   (d) Wan

37. Stint is the opposite of
    (a) Surfeit   (b) Prolix   (c) Meticulous   (d) Splint

38. Which is the odd one out?
    (a) Foam   (b) Mush   (c) Bubbles   (d) Surf

39. Which is the odd one out?
    (a) Pretence   (b) Subterfuge   (c) Moonshine   (d) Reluctance

40. Direct is to Tortuous as Dilatory is to
    (a) Expeditious   (b) Straight   (c) Curved   (d) Circumlocutory

41. Alert is to Loaf as Triumphant is to
    (a) Idle   (b) Cuisine   (c) Prostrate   (d) Elated

42. Which is the odd one out?
    (a) Stand   (b) Vegetate   (c) Prevail   (d) Subsist

43. What is closest in meaning to Permeable?
    (a) Perforated   (b) Tight   (c) Hermetic   (d) Sound

44. Unprepossessing is the opposite of
    (a) Plausible (b) Ostentatious (c) Austere (d) Complementary

Finish

Numerical reasoning

This test assesses how easily you think with numbers.

The test consists of numbers which go together in some way to form a series. You have to see how they go together and then choose the next number from the four answers. When you find the correct answer circle, underline it or put a cross through it.

Try these. The first one has been done for you.

Sample questions

1. 1 2 3 4 5   (a)6 (b)7 (c)5 (d)10
2. 12 10 8 6 4   (a)3 (b)2 (c)1 (d)0
3. 2 4 8 16 32   (a)56 (b)72 (c)144 (d)64
4. 3 4 6 9 13   (a)15 (b)18 (c)17 (d)20
5. 1 1 2 3 5   (a)7 (b)10 (c)8 (d)9
6. 729 243 81 27 9   (a)3 (b)4½ (c)6 (d)–18

Answers and explanation

1. (a) There is an ascending series of numbers. Next in line is 6.

2. (b) 2 is taken from the number on the left. 2 from 4 leaves 2.

3. (d) The number is double the previous number. The next is 64.

4. (b) 1 is added, then 2, then 3, then 4 and then 5, to make 18.

5. (c) The number to the right is added to the number on its left to make the next number, so that 5 added to 3 is 8.

6. (a) Each successive number has been divided by three, so 9 divided by 3 is 3.

Now you can start the full test which begins below. You have *10 minutes* to do as much as you can. You must work as accurately as you can and as fast as you can. When you are ready, start the clock and begin.

1. 6 5 4 3 2 ?   (a)8   (b)4   (c)0   (d)1

2. 1 3 5 7 9 ?   (a)8   (b)11   (c)12   (d)13

3. 1/2 1 2 4 8 ?   (a)12   (b)24   (c)16   (d)18

4. 12 10 8 6 4 ?   (a)0   (b)3   (c)2   (d)4

5. 3 5 8 12 17 ?   (a)25   (b)26   (c)22   (d)23

6. 2 2 4 6 10 ?   (a)14   (b)10   (c)20   (d)16

7. 4 8 16 32 64 ?   (a)96   (b)100   (c)128   (d)112

8. 81 27 9 3 1 ?   (a)1/2   (b)1   (c)1/3   (d)1/6

9. 0.1 0.3 0.5 0.7 0.9 ? (a)1.1   (b)0.11   (c)11   (d)0.011

10. 1 4 9 16 25 ?   (a)32   (b)36   (c)48   (d)49

11. 64 49 36 25 ?   (a)12   (b)16   (c)9   (d)20

12. 5 9 17 33 65 ?   (a)101   (b)108   (c)143   (d)129

13. 0 3 8 15 24 ?   (a)36   (b)30   (c)35   (d)31

14. 1 8 27 64 125 ?   (a)250   (b)216   (c)185   (d)196

15. 5 7 11 17 25 ?   (a)35   (b)27   (c)31   (d)39

16. 4 5 7 11 19 ?   (a)33   (b)27   (c)37   (d)35

17. 0 3 2 5 4 ?   (a)8   (b)7   (c)9   (d)6

18. 0 8 8 16 24 ?   (a)40   (b)24   (c)32   (d)48

19. 2 5 11 23 47 ?   (a)80   (b)95   (c)92   (d)101

20. 10 25 12 30 14 ?   (a)16   (b)50   (c)24   (d)35

21. 3 9 6 15 9 ?   (a)8   (b)15   (c)12   (d)21

22. 50 40 100 90 150 ?   (a)200   (b)180   (c)140   (d)300

23. 2 4 4 16 16 ?   (a)32   (b)64   (c)24   (d)196

24. 15 9 24 33 57 ?   (a)80   (b)90   (c)89   (d)48

Finish

Perceptual reasoning

This test looks at how easily you can reason with symbols and shapes.

After each question there are four answers and, when you have found the correct answer, put a circle around, underline or cross out, your choice. The first one has been completed for you.

Sample questions

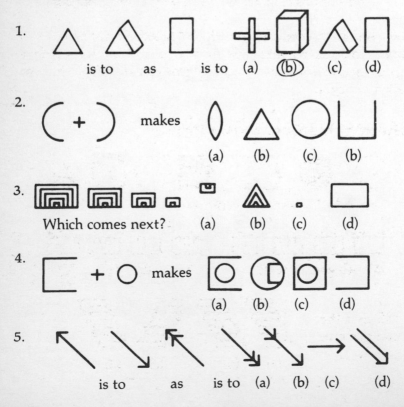

1.

is to   as   is to   (a)   (b)   (c)   (d)

2.

(+)   makes   (a)   (b)   (c)   (b)

3.

Which comes next?   (a)   (b)   (c)   (d)

4.

+ ○   makes   (a)   (b)   (c)   (d)

5.

is to   as   is to   (a)   (b)   (c)   (d)

Answers and explanation

1. (b)   The triangle becomes three-dimensional with a triangle as the facing side. In the same way, the rectangular shape becomes three-dimensional and has the same rectangular facing.

2. (c)   The two half circles put together make a circle, so the answer is (c).

3. (c)   On each occasion the shape is reduced in size and the number of lines is also reduced.

4. (a)   Answer (a) contains both parts. None of the other answers can be correct because the parts are a different size or are different in some way from the original parts.

5. (a)   The figure (like an arrow) is the same and turned around to be opposite in just the same way as the first pair.

Now you can start the full test which begins below. You have *10 minutes* to do as much as you can. You must work as accurately as you can and as fast as you can. When you are ready, start the clock and begin.

Testing perceptual reasoning

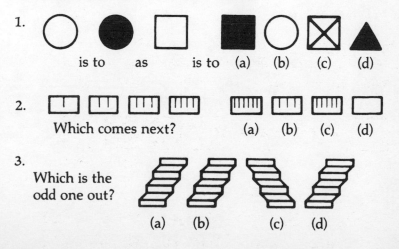

1.

is to   as   is to   (a)   (b)   (c)   (d)

2.

Which comes next?   (a)   (b)   (c)   (d)

3.

Which is the
odd one out?

(a)   (b)   (c)   (d)

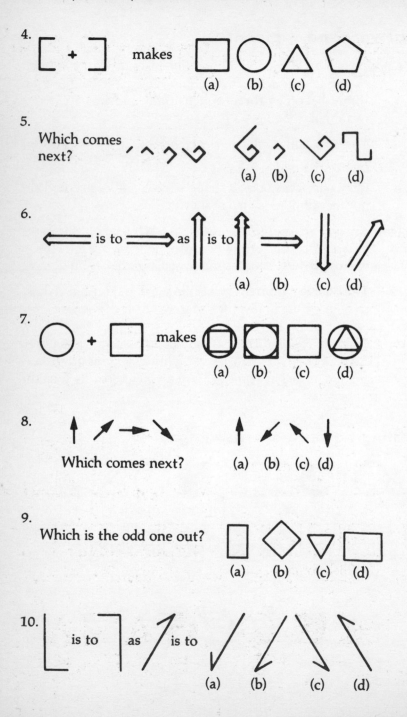

4. [+] makes □(a) ○(b) △(c) ⬠(d)

5. Which comes next?
(a) (b) (c) (d)

6. ⟸ is to ⟹ as ‖ is to
(a) (b) (c) (d)

7. ○ + □ makes
(a) (b) (c) (d)

8. Which comes next?
(a) (b) (c) (d)

9. Which is the odd one out?
(a) (b) (c) (d)

10. is to as is to
(a) (b) (c) (d)

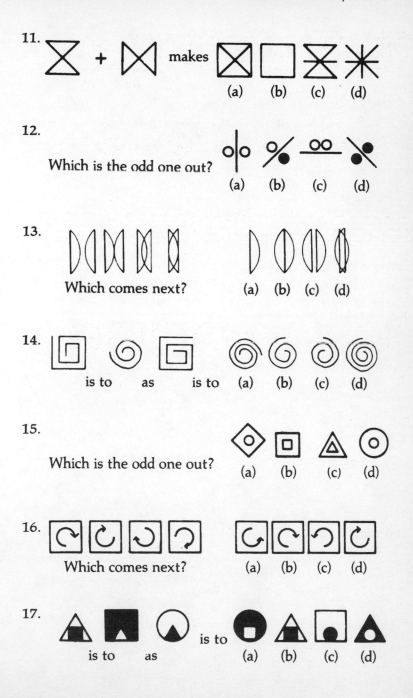

11.

⊠ + ⋈ makes ⊠ ▢ ⋈ ✳
                 (a) (b) (c) (d)

12.

Which is the odd one out?
        (a) (b) (c) (d)

13.

Which comes next?
       (a) (b) (c) (d)

14.

is to   as   is to (a) (b) (c) (d)

15.

Which is the odd one out?
       (a) (b) (c) (d)

16.

Which comes next?
       (a) (b) (c) (d)

17.

is to   as   is to (a) (b) (c) (d)

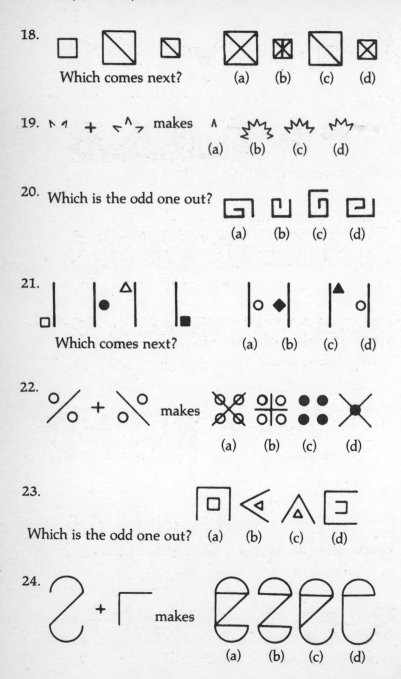

18.

Which comes next?   (a)   (b)   (c)   (d)

19. ⋏⋏ + ⋏⋏⋏ makes ⋏   (a)   (b)   (c)   (d)

20. Which is the odd one out?   (a)   (b)   (c)   (d)

21.

Which comes next?   (a)   (b)   (c)   (d)

22.

% + makes   (a)   (b)   (c)   (d)

23.

Which is the odd one out?   (a)   (b)   (c)   (d)

24.

+ makes   (a)   (b)   (c)   (d)

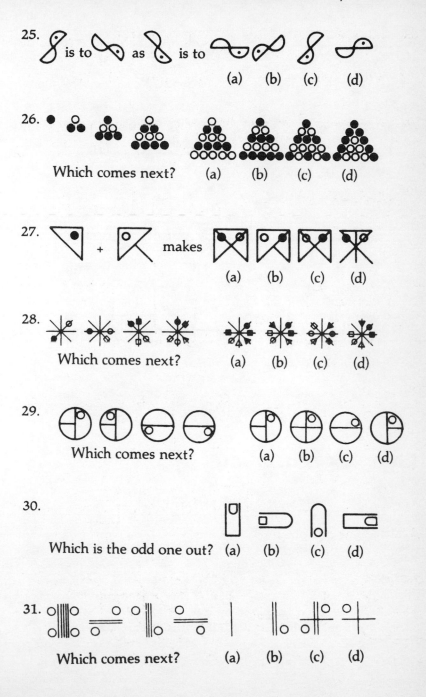

25. is to as is to (a) (b) (c) (d)

26. Which comes next? (a) (b) (c) (d)

27. + makes (a) (b) (c) (d)

28. Which comes next? (a) (b) (c) (d)

29. Which comes next? (a) (b) (c) (d)

30. Which is the odd one out? (a) (b) (c) (d)

31. Which comes next? (a) (b) (c) (d)

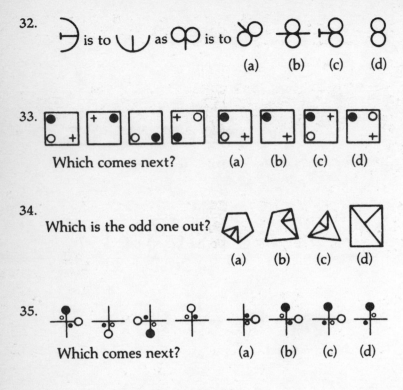

32. ⊃ is to ⋃ as ⋈ is to   (a)   (b)   (c)   (d)

33. Which comes next?   (a)   (b)   (c)   (d)

34. Which is the odd one out?   (a)   (b)   (c)   (d)

35. Which comes next?   (a)   (b)   (c)   (d)

Finish

Complex reasoning

This test sees how well you can apply logic to widening evidence.

In this test you are given six different shapes each of which is shown as white, crossed or black. There are 18 possible answers. These are set out on the next page. In each problem, you have to find out which TWO shapes come next in order of the sequence. Then, select the correct two answers from the 18 possibilities that are provided for you. Write the answers in the correct order in the space provided. The first of the examples has been done to show you how.

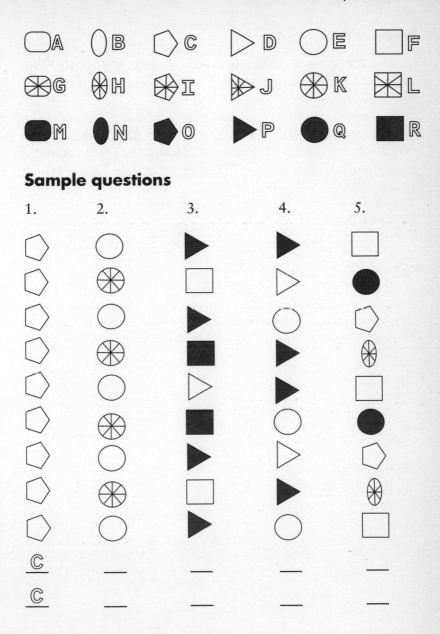

Sample questions

Answers

In example 2, the sequence is always a circle alternately plain and crossed. Therefore, the next circle is crossed and then plain. The answer is 'K E'.

In example 3, the sequence is triangle, square, triangle, square, and so on. The other sequence is plain, two black, plain, two black, and so on. The answer is a square, then a triangle, and also black then white. Therefore, you should have written 'R D'.

In example 4, the sequence is two triangles then a circle. The answer is 'D P'.

The answer to example 5 is 'Q C'. The sequence is plain, black, plain, crossed, while the sequence of shapes is 'square, circle, polygon, lozenge'.

You have 15 minutes for this test. With each problem you must find two letters and these must be in the correct order, otherwise they will not count. When you are ready, start the clock and begin.

Complex reasoning test

1.   2.   3.   4.   5.

6.   7.   8.   9.   10.

A   B   C   D   E   F

G   H   I   J   K   L

M   N   O   P   Q   R

11.   12.   13.   14.   15.

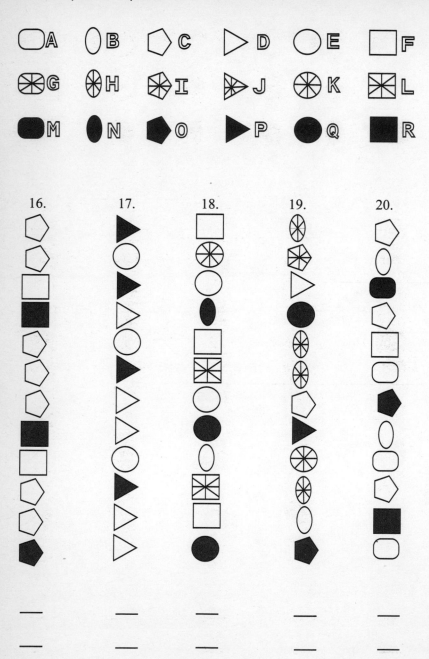

A   B   C   D   E   F

G   H   I   J   K   L

M   N   O   P   Q   R

21.	22.	23.	24.	25.

—   —   —   —   —

—   —   —   —   —

Finish

Spatial ability

This test explores how easily you can 'see' and manipulate shapes and figures in space. Here you are not being asked to reason with the shapes but to move them through three dimensions as quickly as you can.

You are to answer each question with a 'Y' for yes or possibly yes or 'N' for definitely no.

There are two types of question and here are some examples:

Type 1
Here you are given a plan of the three dimensional shape as if you were making it from a sheet of cardboard.

For instance, if you unfolded the cube

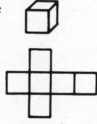

the shape you would get would be:

Following this plan are three or four models and you are to state whether or not each shape can be made from the plan.

Type 2
This time you are given two shapes and the second is to be taken away from the first. Following these two shapes are three or four other shapes and you are to state whether or not this shape could be left.

Sample questions

Put a circle, underline or cross through the correct answer for each question.

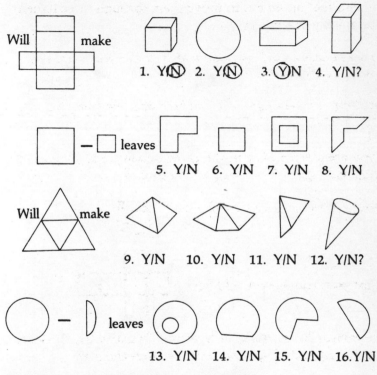

Will [ ] make   1. Y/N 2. Y/N 3. Y/N 4. Y/N?

[ ] – [ ] leaves   5. Y/N 6. Y/N 7. Y/N 8. Y/N

Will make   9. Y/N 10. Y/N 11. Y/N 12. Y/N?

○ –) leaves   13. Y/N 14. Y/N 15. Y/N 16. Y/N

Answers to sample questions

1. N	9. Y
2. N	10. N
3. Y	11. Y
4. Y	12. N
5. Y	13. N
6. N	14. Y
7. Y	15. N
8. N	16. N

Check your answers. If you have made a mistake look at the question again to see, if you can, where you went wrong.

Now you can start the full test which begins below. You can have *10 minutes* to do as much as you can. You must work as accurately as you can and as fast as you can. When you are ready, start the clock and begin.

Testing spatial ability

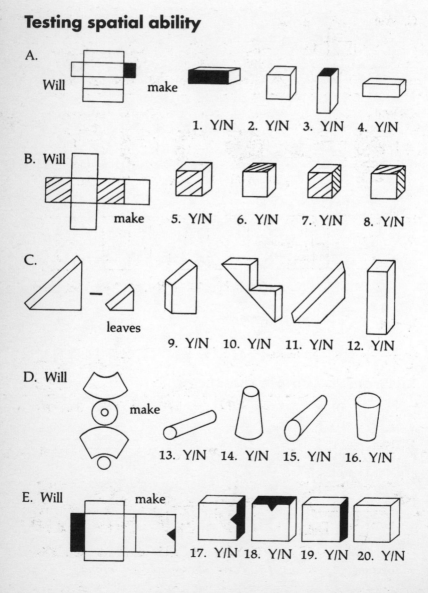

A.

Will   make

1. Y/N   2. Y/N   3. Y/N   4. Y/N

B. Will   make

5. Y/N   6. Y/N   7. Y/N   8. Y/N

C.   leaves

9. Y/N   10. Y/N   11. Y/N   12. Y/N

D. Will   make

13. Y/N   14. Y/N   15. Y/N   16. Y/N

E. Will   make

17. Y/N   18. Y/N   19. Y/N   20. Y/N

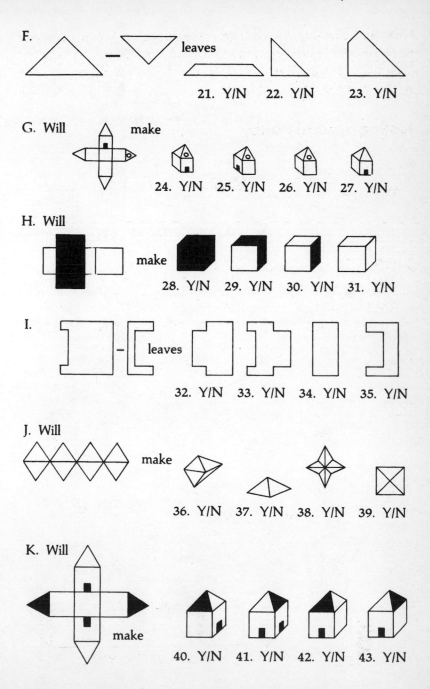

F. △ − ▽ leaves

21. Y/N   22. Y/N   23. Y/N

G. Will [pencil shape] make

24. Y/N   25. Y/N   26. Y/N   27. Y/N

H. Will [net shape] make

28. Y/N   29. Y/N   30. Y/N   31. Y/N

I. [shape] − [shape] leaves

32. Y/N   33. Y/N   34. Y/N   35. Y/N

J. Will [row of triangles] make

36. Y/N   37. Y/N   38. Y/N   39. Y/N

K. Will [cross shape] make

40. Y/N   41. Y/N   42. Y/N   43. Y/N

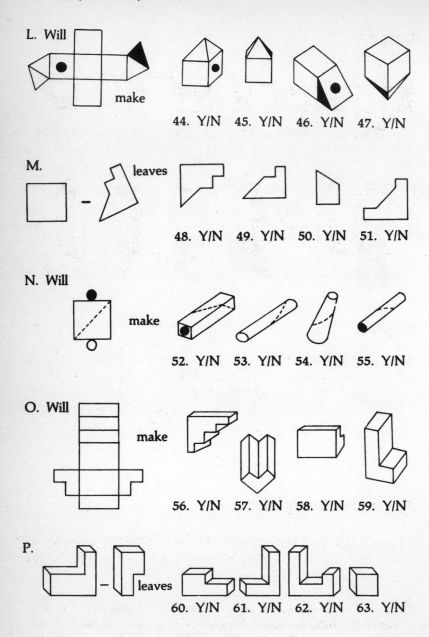

L. Will

make

44. Y/N   45. Y/N   46. Y/N   47. Y/N

M.

□ – leaves

48. Y/N   49. Y/N   50. Y/N   51. Y/N

N. Will

make

52. Y/N   53. Y/N   54. Y/N   55. Y/N

O. Will

make

56. Y/N   57. Y/N   58. Y/N   59. Y/N

P.

– leaves

60. Y/N   61. Y/N   62. Y/N   63. Y/N

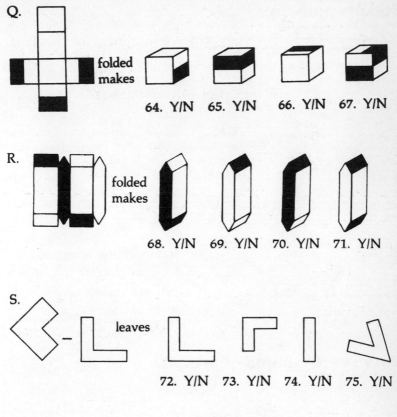

Q.

folded makes

64. Y/N   65. Y/N   66. Y/N   67. Y/N

R.

folded makes

68. Y/N   69. Y/N   70. Y/N   71. Y/N

S.

leaves

72. Y/N   73. Y/N   74. Y/N   75. Y/N

Finish

Technical ability

This test is to find out whether you have a 'feel' for mechanical and technical things. It explores whether or not you find it easy to understand how things work and function.

Each written question has a diagram by it to give you the required information. Choose the correct answer from the choices given. Put a circle around, underline or cross out, the correct answer. The first one has been completed for you.

Sample questions

1.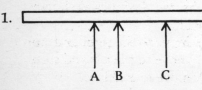
A   B   C

Which arrow will balance
the beam?
(a) A   (b) B   (c) C
(d) all equal

2. P   Q
R

Which chain will hold up the lantern?
(a) P   (b) Q   (c) R   (d) all equal

3.

If the driving wheel goes in
the direction shown, which
way will the second wheel
turn?
(a) either   (b) ⌢   (c) ⌢

Answers to sample questions

1. (b)   The arrow, B, points to a place at the centre of the beam
so that the weight of the beam is distributed equally.

2. (b)   The chain, Q, is holding up the beam from which the
lantern is suspended. Chains P and R could be removed
and the lantern would remain held in just the same way.

3. (c)   As the driving wheel turns clockwise the connecting
chains (or ropes) around the wheels also turn. Because
the connecting chains cross over each other, the second
wheel turns in the opposite direction to the driving
wheel, anticlockwise.

Now you can start the full test which begins on the next page.
You have *10 minutes* to do as much as you can. You must work
as accurately as you can and as fast as you can. When you are
ready, start the clock and begin.

Testing technical ability

1.

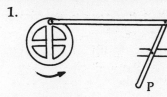

If the wheel rotates as shown,
P will
(a) move to the right and stop
(b) move to the left and stop
(c) move to and fro
(d) none of these

2.

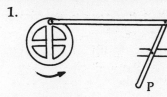

Which arrow will balance the
beam?
(a) A   (b) B   (c) C   (d) D

3.

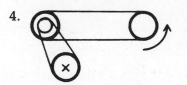

When the two screws are turned
the same amount as shown, the
ball will move towards
(a) F   (b) G   (c) H   (d) J   (e) K

4.

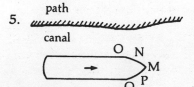

Which way does wheel X move?
(a) either   (b) ⤴   (c) ⤴
(d) stays still

5.

path

canal

To move the boat easily in the
direction shown, the rope would
be best attached to
(a) M   (b) N   (c) O   (d) P
(e) Q

6.

Which nail is most likely to pull
out of the wall?
(a) A   (b) B   (c) C
(d) all equally likely

7.

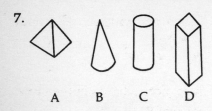

If each block weighs the same, which one will be most difficult to push over?
(a) A   (b) B   (c) C   (d) D

8.

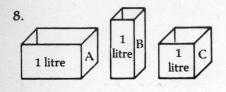

Which tank will cool water fastest?
(a) A   (b) B   (c) C
(d) All equal

9.

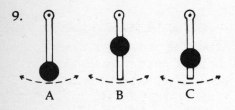

Which pendulum moves slowest?
(a) A   (b) B   (c) C
(d) all equal

10.

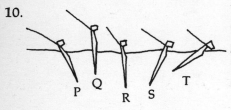

Which tent peg will give the best hold in soft ground?
(a) P   (b) Q   (c) R
(d) S   (e) T

11.

Which weight will be easiest to lift?
(a) A   (b) B   (c) C
(d) all equal

12. If each rope in the above diagram is pulled at the same speed, which load will move slowest?
    (a) A   (b) B   (c) C   (d) all equal

13. Which gear wheel goes in the same direction as the driver?
    (a) X   (b) Y   (c) Z

14. Which gear wheel goes round fastest?
    (a) W   (b) X   (c) Y   (d) Z

15. Where is the cannonball most likely to land?
    (a) A   (b) B   (c) C   (d) D

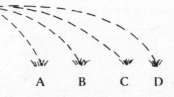

16. 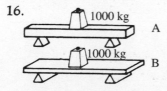 Which plank is most likely to break?
    (a) A   (b) B   (c) either

17. 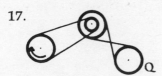 Which way will wheel Q turn?
    (a) ↰   (b) ↱   (c) either

18.

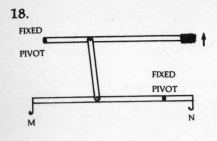

If the handle is moved as
shown, how will the hooks
M and N move?
(a) M up, N down
(b) M down, N up
(c) M up, N up
(d) M down, N down
(e) M up, N still

19.

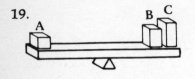

Which box is the heaviest?
(a) A   (b) B   (c) C
(d) all equal

20.

Which way will the black
ball move when struck by the
white ball in the direction
shown?
(a) A   (b) B   (c) C   (d) D

21. The diameter of pulleys A and C is 10cm and pulleys B and
D is 5cm. When pulley A makes a complete turn pulley D
will turn
(a) once   (b) twice   (c) 4 times   (d) 6 times   (e) 8 times

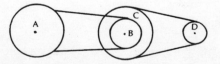

22. If pulley D is the driver, which pulley turns slowest?
(a) A   (b) B   (c) C   (d) all the same

23.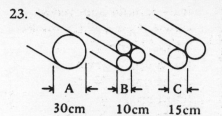

If the drawing is of water pipes, which will carry the most water per metre length?
(a) A   (b) B   (c) C
(d) all equal

24. If the drawing is of electrical cable, which offers the most resistance per metre length?
(a) A   (b) B   (c) C   (d) all equal

25.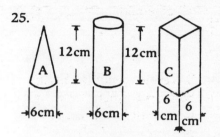

If the blocks are all of the same material, which is the heaviest?
(a) A   (b) B   (c) C
(d) all equal

26. Which has the greatest density?
(a) A   (b) B   (c) C   (d) all equal

27.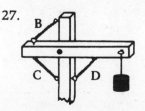

Which chain would support the weight by itself?
(a) any equally   (b) B
(c) C   (d) D

28. Which diagram shows the most likely path of a bomb falling from a moving aeroplane on a calm day?
(a) X   (b) Y   (c) Z

29. 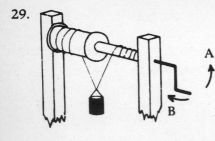 Which way will the handle have to turn to raise the bucket?
(a) A   (b) B   (c) either

30. Which of these would return to its present position when moved slightly?
(a) A   (b) B   (c) neither   (d) both

31. 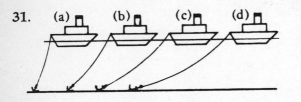 Which boat has the safest anchorage?

32. 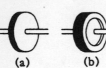 Which shape makes the best flywheel?

(a)   (b)   (c)

33. Where is the pendulum moving fastest?

Finish

Acuity skills

This test is to see how quickly and accurately you can complete clerical tasks. There are two parts to the test.

Each part takes 5 minutes and you must time yourself accurately. The first part is simply sums using the four rules + − × ÷. For example:

35
7+
──
42

Sample questions

1. 26   2. 35   3. 74
   9+   12−   7×
   ──   ──   ──

In the second part you have three names and you are to find which one should come first if they were filed in alphabetical order. Put a cross through it or underline it. For example:

(a) Jones   (b) ~~Jason~~   (c) Joseph

Sample questions

1. (a) Taylor   (b) Tailor   (c) Townsend
2. (a) Deader   (b) Dreader   (c) Dader
3. (a) Wisp   (b) Willow   (c) Wilter

Answers to sample questions

Part 1
1. 35   2. 23   3. 518

Part 2
1. (b)   2. (c)   3. (b)

Check your answers. If you have made a mistake look at the question again to see, if you can, where you went wrong.

You must work as accurately as you can and as fast as you can. You have *5 minutes* only on each part. When you have finished Part 1 go straight on to Part 2. As soon as you are ready, start the clock and begin.

Acuity test 1

Remember you only have *5 minutes* for this part.

1.	24 5+	2.	71 9+	3.	35 69+	4.	45 62+	5.	15 19 23+

6.	26 6×	7.	37 48 35+	8.	49 8×	9.	64 57 62+	10.	48 13–

11.	127 98–	12.	35 9×	13.	7) 364	14.	28 364 479+	15.	3) 369

16.	67 12+	17.	47 5×	18.	249 158–	19.	8) 584	20.	6016 739–

21. 279   22. 135   23.   37   24.   25. 924

     686   36–   9×   12)‾1452‾   536–

     755+   ‾‾‾   ‾‾‾   ‾‾‾

     ‾‾‾

26. 612   27. 26   28. 23   29. 24   30. 916

     387–   15   83+   8×   158–

     ‾‾‾   83+   ‾‾‾   ‾‾‾   ‾‾‾

                 ‾‾‾

31. 54   32. 67   33. 217   34. 43   35.

     36+   29+   138–   11×   6)‾3528‾

     ‾‾‾   ‾‾‾   ‾‾‾   ‾‾‾

Acuity test 2

Put a cross through the name to be filed first. Remember, you have only 5 minutes for this part.

	(a)	(b)	(c)
1.	Able	Abel	Abbel
2.	Tango	Tanker	Tabber
3.	Swift	Switch	Stuck
4.	Dean	Deal	Drift
5.	Frant	French	Freak
6.	Tranter	Truck	Tramper
7.	Grant	Gant	Great
8.	Willis	Wiltshire	Wilter
9.	Simons	Simkins	Simmons
10.	Stanley	Sturdy	Straemer
11.	Foster	Forster	Fortnum
12.	Yarrow	Yaught	Yammer
13.	Pear	Pearce	Pearson
14.	Burch	Birch	Brunch
15.	Fox	Fotse	Foray

16. (a) Hamilton	(b) Harding	(c) Hammer
17. (a) Gough	(b) Guntler	(c) Goff
18. (a) Pear	(b) Peirs	(c) Pedlar
19. (a) Brown	(b) Browne	(c) Brownne
20. (a) Milton	(b) Miller	(c) Milstone
21. (a) Delafield	(b) Deldafield	(c) Delderfield
22. (a) Johnson	(b) Johnstone	(c) Johnston
23. (a) Jackron	(b) Jackson	(c) Jackman
24. (a) Phillips	(b) Philips	(c) Phillippes
25. (a) Crow	(b) Crout	(c) Crove
26. (a) Mackie	(b) Mackensie	(c) Macky
27. (a) Young	(b) Younger	(c) Youngest
28. (a) Crispin	(b) Crist	(c) Crump
29. (a) Wober	(b) Waller	(c) Walters
30. (a) Katz	(b) Katin	(c) Kaarl
31. (a) Davis	(b) Davies	(c) Davit
32. (a) Mordecai	(b) Morden	(c) Mortimer
33. (a) Butler	(b) Buwer	(c) Butcher
34. (a) Stratford	(b) Stafford	(c) Strafford
35. (a) Wallis	(b) Wallace	(c) Warris
36. (a) Pearson	(b) Pearston	(c) Pearstron
37. (a) Rhostra	(b) Rodda	(c) Rhonda
38. (a) Tailor	(b) Taylor	(c) Tail
39. (a) Carter	(b) Carver	(c) Carstair
40. (a) Zuiler	(b) Zweger	(c) Zueeter
41. (a) Stanine	(b) Stanton	(c) Stanned
42. (a) Able	(b) Abel	(c) Abbot
43. (a) Travers	(b) Traverse	(c) Travart
44. (a) Quintcy	(b) Quinton	(c) Quintel
45. (a) Gromner	(b) Grommer	(c) Gronner
46. (a) Rabbis	(b) Rabbes	(c) Rabast
47. (a) Norving	(b) Norway	(c) Norwyn
48. (a) Wrighton	(b) Whiton	(c) Whitton
49. (a) Crabbes	(b) Crates	(c) Crabs
50. (a) Zeron	(b) Zero	(c) Zerox

51.	(a) Cane	(b) Caine	(c) Cayne
52.	(a) Rushton	(b) Tushton	(c) Riston
53.	(a) Noord	(b) Nourd	(c) Nord
54.	(a) Sarid	(b) Sarit	(c) Sarip
55.	(a) Constable	(b) Constabulary	(c) Constible
56.	(a) Farringdon	(b) Faringone	(c) Farrington
57.	(a) Gribble	(b) Grimble	(c) Gristle
58.	(a) Saul	(b) Tall	(c) Paul
59.	(a) Yacht	(b) Yapped	(c) Yaed
60.	(a) Lines	(b) Lyes	(c) Linde
61.	(a) Rapport	(b) Robot	(c) Redditch
62.	(a) Clore	(b) Clare	(c) Clair
63.	(a) Zeus	(b) Zude	(c) Zoo
64.	(a) Bable	(b) Able	(c) Abbot
65.	(a) Right	(b) Plight	(c) Sight
66.	(a) Carryon	(b) Carrion	(c) Clarion
67.	(a) Wavey	(b) Wacey	(c) Wackey
68.	(a) Ingrid	(b) Ingret	(c) Ingreed
69.	(a) Derry	(b) Derron	(c) Derret
70.	(a) Querible	(b) Queastor	(c) Quest

Finish

Coding

This test sees how accurately and quickly you can exchange bits of information from one form to another.

In this test you are given a number and letter that relates to Table 1. From these you locate a symbol. Then you look up the symbol in Table 2 and find a new number and letter. You then look up the new number and letter in Table 3 to find a large, capital letter.

	Table 1				Table 2					Table 3				
1	◆				5	6	7	8		h	g	f	e	
2	○	⌘			●	◆	○	♌	e			T	5	
3	♏	⊠	⋇		⌘	□	⋇	f			E	O	6	
4	♌	●	☼	□		☼	♏	g		A	S	H	7	
	a	b	c	d			⊠	h		U	L	R	C	8

For example, look at the pairs '4a–3a–3b–2b'. '4a' gives the symbol '♌' in Table 1. This is '8e' in Table 2. In Table 3 '8e' gives the letter 'C'. Then take the next pair, '3a'. Using the tables as before, this gives the letter 'L'. Then do the same with the pairs '3b' and '2b'. All the letters will have spelt a word. You have to write the answer clearly in the space provided.

Look at the questions below. The first has been done to show you how.

Sample questions

Answer:

1. 4a–3a–3b–2b   CLUE

2. 4d–2a–1a–4b   _____

3. 3a–2b–4b–4b–2b–3c   _____

Answers

The answer to number 2 is 'SHOT'. The answer to number 3 is 'LETTER'.

When you are ready, start the full test. You have 8 minutes. You must work accurately and quickly. When you are ready, start the clock and begin.

Coding test

	Table 1		Table 2		Table 3

Table 1

1 ◆
2 ○ ⌘
3 ♏ ⊠ ⌘
4 ♌ ● ☼ □
5 ❖ ♋ ♎ ⚹ ♒
6 ☯ ⊠ ♊ ☾ ♈ ♱
   a b c d e f

Table 2

7 8 9 10 11 12
⊠ ♈ ♱ ○ ☾ ☼ g
   ● ◆ ♌ ♏ ❖ h
   ♊ ♓ ⌘ □ i
      ⚹ ⊠ ♋ j
         ♒ ☯ k
            ♎ l

Table 3

l k j i h g
            T 7
         C R 8
      L S E 9
   B H P A 10
T D MU F 11
I G O N Y W 12

Answer:

1.   6a–5b   _____
2.   5c–4d   _____
3.   5d–5c–5e   _____
4.   3b–5c–6a   _____
5.   2a–4a–5e   _____
6.   6d–5b–6e   _____
7.   6d–6c–5a   _____
8.   1a–3a–2b   _____
9.   3c–3a–5d   _____
10. 3b–5b–4c   _____

From question 11 use Tables 4, 5 and 6.

	Table 4			*Table 5*			*Table 6*	

Table 4

6	◆				
5	○	✵			
4	♏	⊡	♓		
3	♌	●	✿	□	
2	❖	♋	♎	✗	♒
1	☺	⊠	♊	☾	♂	✝
	a	b	c	d	e	f

Table 5

	7	8	9	10	11	12	
	♎	○	☾	♓	✻	□	l
		●	⊡	♋	◆	♌	k
			⊠	♂	✝	♊	j
				♏	❖	✗	i
					♒	☺	h
						✿	g

Table 6

g h i j k l
T 7
C R 8
L S E 9
B H P A 10
T D MU K 11
I G O N Y W 12

Answer:

11.	1b–2d–3d	_____
12.	4b–2b–4c	_____
13.	5b–3c–2c	_____
14.	1c–3c–2b	_____
15.	4a–4c–5a	_____
16.	3a–1d–2c	_____
17.	1c–2d–2a	_____
18.	2c–6a–1a	_____
19.	2b–1b–3a	_____
20.	2d–4c–5b	_____

From question 21 use Tables 7, 8 and 9.

	Table 7				
1	♊				
2	✦	♋			
3	☯	◆	⊠		
4	♌	●	✿	□	
5	♐	♎	○	⌘	♒
6	☾	♈	♁	♏	⊡	♓
	a	b	c	d	e	f

Table 8

9	12	10	11	7	8
⌘	□	♋	♎	☾	♓ h
●	○	⊠	◆	♌	j
⊠	✿	♁	♊		i
		☯	♏	♐	l
		✦	♒		g
			♈		k

Table 9

k	g	l	i	j	h
				F	9
			I	G	12
		L	S	E	10
	B	H P	A		11
U	T	C R	D		7
O	N	Y V	K M		8

Answer:

21. 3a–5b–6c–4a   _____

22. 6d–4b–6a–5a   _____

23. 4d–3b–6a–6d   _____

24. 6e–3c–2a–6f   _____

25. 4c–2b–3b–6b   _____

26. 4d–5a–6a–4c   _____

27. 3a–6b–4d–2a–5c   _____

28. 6c–5b–1a–6a–3c   _____

29. 6e–3c–5b–5e–4a   _____

30. 6a–3b–2b–5e–6c–4c   _____

Finish

Analytical ability

In this test we are looking at the way in which you can analyse information and draw logical conclusions. You are to use only the information given.

You may find it easier to have a piece of scrap paper when you tackle this test. There are two types of question and here are examples of both:

Type 1

Here you are given some information and asked to answer the question following using the facts as they have been given. Put a cross through the answer you believe to be correct. The example has been answered to show you how to proceed.

Jean and Janet like skipping. Jane and Jean wear glasses.

Who might break her glasses while skipping? (Jean, Janet, Jane)

Type 2

Here you are given a statement in bold type and four facts. You have to choose the two facts that are necessary to make the statement true. Only two facts taken together are essential. Put a cross through the letters of the two facts. The example has been done for you.

Hightown is north of Lowtown.

(a) Lowtown is south of Midtown
(b) Hightown is north of Centerville
(c) Centerville is south of Midtown
(d) Midtown is south of Hightown

Here are some examples for you to try.

Sample questions

Jim is taller than Jack. John is taller than Jim.

1. Who is tallest? (Jim, Jack, John)
2. Who is shortest? (Jim, Jack, John)

Anne and Albert like dogs. Alfred and Augusta like horses. Anne and Augusta are tall.

3. Who was the tall girl out riding? (Anne, Albert, Alfred, Augusta)

Anville is north of Deeside.

4. (a) Deeside is south of Beeside.
   (b) Anville is north of Beeside.
   (c) Beeside is east of Seatown.
   (d) Deeside is south-west of Seatown.

Steve is tall and dark.

5. (a) Steve and Paul are tall.
   (b) Paul and Percy are not dark.
   (c) Percy and Ernest are not tall.
   (d) Ernest and Steve are not fair.

Answers to sample questions

1. John. With this type of question it can be helpful to write down the information you are given in a way that allows you to see the problem more clearly. Thus, 'Jim is taller than Jack' so:
   Jim
   Jack
       and 'John is taller than Jim' so:
   John
   Jim
   Jack thus, John is the tallest.

2. Jack.

3. Augusta. Again, it helps to lay out the information in a table or diagram, for example:

	dogs	horses	tall
Anne	yes		yes
Albert	yes		
Alfred		yes	
Augusta		yes	yes

It is easy to see that it could only have been Augusta who was the tall girl out riding.

4. (a) and (b). Laying out the information, it looks like this:

Anville (north of Beeside)

Seatown   Beeside (east of Seatown)

Deeside (south of Beeside) (south west of Seatown)

5. (a) and (d). In this problem people are either tall or short and either fair and therefore not dark or not fair and therefore dark. In (a) Steve is said to be tall. In (d) he is said to be 'not fair', therefore, he must be dark.

Now you can start the full test which begins on the next page. You have *10 minutes* to do as much as you can. You must work as accurately as you can and as fast as you can. When you are ready, start the clock and begin.

Testing analytical ability

Put a cross through the correct answer(s). (Remember that two answers are required for Type 2 questions.)

Lowfield is bigger than Newerfield. Middlefield is bigger than Lowfield.

1. Which town is biggest? (Lowfield, Newerfield, Middlefield)

Sue and Jennifer are fair. Brian and Robyn are dark. Sue and Robyn are tall.

2. Who is fair and tall? (Sue, Jennifer, Brian, Robyn)

3. Who is tall and dark? (Sue, Jennifer, Brian, Robyn)

Martha is playing marbles.

4. (a) Martha is in the marbles team during the summer.
    (b) Martha is in the playground.
    (c) Marbles is played in the playground in summer.
    (d) All the pupils in the playground are playing marbles.

Adam runs faster than Stuart.

5. (a) Swithin is the champion runner.
    (b) Adam can run further than Swithin.
    (c) Adam can run as fast as Swithin.
    (d) Swithin can run faster than Stuart.

Janet, Marcus, Eric and Angela sit in this order in a row left to right. Janet changes places with Eric and then Eric changes places with Marcus.

6. Who is at the right end of the row? (Janet, Marcus, Eric, Angela)
7. Who is to the left of Eric? (Janet, Marcus, Angela)

A group of friends live in a house divided into one flat per floor. Tony is in the flat below Julie and Madeleine is in the flat above Sarah. Sarah is in the flat below Tony and Julie lives with Roger. Peter lives on the top floor.

8. Who is in the bottom flat? (Tony, Julie, Madeleine, Sarah, Peter)
9. Who else shares a flat? (Tony and Madeleine, Sarah and Peter, Tony and Peter, Madeleine and Sarah)

Some of the school choir won book tokens.

10. (a) The whole of Form IV won attendance awards.
    (b) Some who won a book token were also given a certificate.
    (c) The attendance awards were book tokens.
    (d) All who were given a certificate were in the choir.

James is eight years old and half as old as his brother Humphrey. Jenny is two years younger than James and the same number of years older than Mark.

11. Who is the oldest? (James, Humphrey, Jenny, Mark)

12. Who is the youngest? (James, Humphrey, Jenny, Mark)

13. How old is Mark? (1, 2, 3, 4, 5, 6, 7, 8, 9)

14. How much younger is Jenny than Humphrey? (4, 6, 7, 8, 9, 10, 12 years)

Five cars had a race. The Honda beat the Rover but couldn't overtake the Astra. The Renault failed to overtake the Granada but beat the Astra.

15. Which car came last? (Honda, Rover, Astra, Renault, Granada)

16. Which car came third? (Honda, Rover, Astra, Renault, Granada)

Jane can play the piano but not the flute while Jeremy plays the violin and the flute. Shelley plays the violin but not the piano and Josephine plays the flute but not the violin.

17. If each child plays two of the three instruments, which one is likely to be similar to Jeremy? (Shelley, Jane, Josephine)

A man drove from Appleby to Trytown. Shortly after passing through Ester he stopped for coffee at Broughton which was the halfway point on his journey.

18. Which is the longest distance? (Appleby to Ester, Ester to Trytown, Broughton to Trytown, Ester to Broughton)

Fifty candidates sat the examination.

19. (a) Twenty candidates answered under half the questions.
    (b) There were ten failures in the examination.
    (c) Over half the questions were answered by thirty candidates.
    (d) Forty candidates were successful.

Onetown is north-east of Threetown.

20. (a) Onetown is two miles north of Twotown.
    (b) Twotown is two miles west of Fourtown.
    (c) Threetown is two miles west of Twotown.
    (d) Fourtown is south-east of Onetown.

Sunday was wetter than Monday but sunnier than Saturday.

21. Which day was wettest? (Saturday, Sunday, Monday)

Today is a Tuesday.

22. (a) June began on a Wednesday this year.
    (b) Three days ago it was Saturday.
    (c) It is 21 June today.
    (d) 22 June was on a Tuesday last year.

Six families live in a three-storey block of flats. They are numbered so that even numbers have a door on the right and odd numbers a door on the left. Numbers 1 and 2 are on the ground floor; 3 and 4 on the first floor and 5 and 6 on the top floor. The Laskeys have a door on the right and are between two families.

23. Where do the Laskeys live? (1, 2, 3, 4, 5, 6)

In the same block, the Epsons live in an even-numbered flat with the Raymonds below them. The Rowans live opposite the Laskeys and the Roses and Ewells both live opposite families with different initials.

24. Where do the Roses live? (1, 2, 3, 4, 5, 6)

25. Who lives opposite the Raymonds? (Epsons, Rowans, Laskeys, Roses, Ewells)

26. Who is over the Laskeys? (Epsons, Raymonds, Rowans, Roses, Ewells)

27. Who is at number 1? (Epsons, Raymonds, Rowans, Laskeys, Roses, Ewells)

28. Who is at number 6? (Epsons, Raymonds, Rowans, Laskeys, Roses, Ewells)

Percy Howard and his wife, Mary, and one of his twin daughters live on the corner of Apple Walk and Peartree Road. They also have two sons (Jack and Geoff) who live either side of them. Jack is married to Abigail and they live in Peartree Road. Susan shares her name with her sister-in-law who still lives at home. Stephanie is divorced from David and lives in the next town but visits her brother and his two sons in Apple Walk regularly. All the immediate family have been mentioned.

29. Who lives in Apple Walk? (David and Stephanie, Geoff and Stephanie, Geoff and Susan, Susan and Jack)

30. Who lives with Mr and Mrs Howard? (Mary, Abigail, Susan, Stephanie)

31. Who are the twins? (Mary and Susan, Susan and Stephanie, Abigail and Stephanie, Abigail and Mary)

Finish

Marking and interpreting the tests

For each question there is one acceptable answer. In each test count one point where your answer matches the answer given in these results. At the end of each test count the number of correct marks that you have gained. This is your raw test score.

When you have found your raw score compare it with the grading tables under the answers. This is your guide for that particular test. The group which has been used to produce these comparisons is slightly above the average for the whole country. All have, or confidently expect to have, at least two GCSEs (or GCEs) at grade C or above. These grades can then be drawn on the main chart on page 69.

Verbal reasoning: Answers

1. (a)	12. (d)	23. (c)	34. (a)
2. (b)	13. (d)	24. (c)	35. (c)
3. (d)	14. (c)	25. (c)	36. (d)
4. (c)	15. (a)	26. (b)	37. (a)
5. (b)	16. (b)	27. (d)	38. (b)
6. (a)	17. (d)	28. (a)	39. (d)
7. (b)	18. (a)	29. (a)	40. (a)
8. (c)	19. (d)	30. (d)	41. (c)
9. (d)	20. (c)	31. (a)	42. (c)
10. (a)	21. (b)	32. (d)	43. (a)
11. (c)	22. (b)	33. (c)	44. (b)

Grades

A score of 30 or over	grade A
26–29	grade B
23–25	grade C
19–22	grade D
15–18	grade E
14 or under	grade F

Numerical reasoning: Answers

1. (d)	7. (c)	13. (c)	19. (b)
2. (b)	8. (c)	14. (b)	20. (d)
3. (c)	9. (a)	15. (a)	21. (d)
4. (c)	10. (b)	16. (d)	22. (c)
5. (d)	11. (b)	17. (b)	23. (d)
6. (d)	12. (d)	18. (a)	24. (b)

Grades

A score of 20 or over   grade A
15–19   grade B
12–14   grade C
9–11   grade D
4–8   grade E
3 or under   grade F

Perceptual reasoning: Answers

1. (a)	10. (b)	19. (c)	28. (d)
2. (c)	11. (a)	20. (b)	29. (a)
3. (c)	12. (c)	21. (d)	30. (c)
4. (a)	13. (d)	22. (a)	31. (a)
5. (a)	14. (b)	23. (d)	32. (d)
6. (c)	15. (a)	24. (c)	33. (a)
7. (b)	16. (b)	25. (b)	34. (d)
8. (d)	17. (d)	26. (b)	35. (b)
9. (c)	18. (d)	27. (c)	

Grades

A score of 30 or over   grade A
27–29   grade B
24–26   grade C
21–23   grade D
18–20   grade E
17 or under   grade F

Complex reasoning: Answers

1. P	2. F	3. H	4. P	5. K
P	E	D	P	E
6. E	7. E	8. B	9. D	10. E
E	R	C	E	N
11. N	12. K	13. H	14. D	15. F
D	C	I	N	F
16. F	17. D	18. E	19. J	20. C
F	E	H	K	B
21. P	22. I	23. L	24. D	25. I
R	C	J	M	P

Grades

A raw score of 21 or over grade A
17–20 grade B
12–16 grade C
8–11 grade D
4–7 grade E
3 or under grade F

Spatial ability: Answers

1. N	21. Y	40. Y	60. N
2. N	22. Y	41. N	61. N
3. Y	23. N	42. N	62. N
4. Y	24. N	43. Y	63. Y
5. Y	25. Y	44. Y	64. Y
6. Y	26. N	45. N	65. Y
7. N	27. Y	46. N	66. Y
8. N	28. N	47. Y	67. N
9. Y	29. N	48. N	68. Y
10. N	30. Y	49. Y	69. Y
11. Y	31. N	50. N	70. N
12. N	32. N	51. N	71. N
13. N	33. Y	52. N	72. N
14. Y	34. N	53. N	73. Y

15. N	35. N	54. N	74. N
16. N	36. Y	55. Y	75. N
17. Y	37. N	56. N	
18. Y	38. N	57. Y	
19. Y	39. Y	58. Y	
20. Y		59. N	

Grades

A score of 60 or over grade A
            51–59 grade B
            44–50 grade C
            37–43 grade D
            27–36 grade E
   26 or under grade F

Technical ability: Answers

1. (c)	10. (d)	18. (a)	26. (d)
2. (b)	11. (c)	19. (a)	27. (c)
3. (c)	12. (c)	20. (b)	28. (b)
4. (b)	13. (b)	21. (c)	29. (a)
5. (b)	14. (a)	22 (a)	30. (b)
6. (c)	15. (c)	23. (a)	31. (d)
7. (a)	16. (b)	24. (b)	32. (b)
8. (a)	17. (a)	25. (c)	33. (c)
9. (a)			

Grades

A score of 29 or over grade A
            26–28 grade B
            22–25 grade C
            18–21 grade D
            14–17 grade E
   13 or under grade F

Acuity skills: Answers

Part 1

1. 29	2. 80	3. 104	4. 107	5. 57
6. 156	7. 120	8. 392	9. 183	10. 35
11. 29	12. 315	13. 52	14. 871	15. 123
16. 79	17. 235	18. 91	19. 73	20. 5277
21. 1720	22. 99	23. 333	24. 121	25. 388
26. 225	27. 124	28. 106	29. 192	30. 758
31. 90	32. 96	33. 79	34. 473	35. 588

Part 2

1. (c)	16. (a)	31. (b)	46. (c)	61. (a)
2. (c)	17. (c)	32. (a)	47. (a)	62. (c)
3. (c)	18. (a)	33. (c)	48. (b)	63. (a)
4. (b)	19. (a)	34. (b)	49. (a)	64. (c)
5. (a)	20. (b)	35. (b)	50. (b)	65. (b)
6. (c)	21. (a)	36. (a)	51. (b)	66. (b)
7. (b)	22. (a)	37. (c)	52. (c)	67. (b)
8. (a)	23. (c)	38. (c)	53. (a)	68. (c)
9. (b)	24. (b)	39. (c)	54. (a)	69. (c)
10. (a)	25. (b)	40. (c)	55. (a)	70. (b)
11. (b)	26. (b)	41. (a)	56. (b)	
12. (c)	27. (a)	42. (c)	57. (a)	
13. (a)	28. (a)	43. (c)	58. (c)	
14. (b)	29. (b)	44. (a)	59. (a)	
15. (c)	30. (c)	45. (b)	60. (c)	

Add the score from Part 1 to the score from Part 2.

Grades

A score of 74 or over	grade A
66–73	grade B
53–65	grade C
40–52	grade D
32–39	grade E
31 or under	grade F

Coding: Answers

1. GO	11. LOW	21. BACK
2. IN	12. SPA	22. TIDY
3. BIT	13. KIT	23. GRIT
4. DIG	14. NIP	24. PLUM
5. APT	15. BAR	25. HERO
6. FOR	16. YET	26. MYTH
7. FLY	17. NOD	27. BOGUS
8. SUM	18. TUG	28. CAVIL
9. HUB	19. PLY	29. PLANK
10. DOW	20. OAK	30. DRENCH

Grades
A raw score of 24 or over   grade A
19–23   grade B
13–18   grade C
7–12   grade D
4–6   grade E
3 or under   grade F

Analytical ability: Answers

On the questions where two answers were required, both answers must be given correctly to score a point.

1. Middlefield	10. (b) and (d)	21. Sunday
2. Sue	11. Humphrey	22. (a) and (c)
3. Robyn	12. Mark	23. 4
4. (b) and (d)	13. 4	24. 5
5. (c) and (d)	14. 10 years	25. Ewells
6. Angela	15. Rover	26. Epsons
7. Marcus	16. Astra	27. Ewells
8. Sarah	17. Shelley	28. Epsons
9. Tony and Madeleine	18. Ester to Trytown	29. Geoff and Susan
	19. (b) and (d)	30. Susan
	20. (a) and (c)	31. Susan and Stephanie

Grades

A score of 23 or over	grade A
20–22	grade B
16–19	grade C
11–15	grade D
8–10	grade E
7 or under	grade F

Your abilities profile chart

Transfer your grades from pages 63 to 68 on to this chart.

Verbal reasoning	Numerical reasoning	Perceptual reasoning	Complex reasoning	Spatial ability	Technical ability	Acuity skills	Coding	Analytical ability
A	A	A	A	A	A	A	A	A
B	B	B	B	B	B	B	B	B
C	C	C	C	C	C	C	C	C
D	D	D	D	D	D	D	D	D
E	E	E	E	E	E	E	E	E
F	F	F	F	F	F	F	F	F
Verbal reasoning	Numerical reasoning	Perceptual reasoning	Complex reasoning	Spatial ability	Technical ability	Acuity skills	Coding	Analytical ability

Interpreting your ability results

The profile graph of your ability test results tells you two different things. First it gives you an idea of the general level of your abilities and second, an idea of your particular strengths and weaknesses.

The grades are based on a sample of people, most of whom had gained some kind of academic qualification ranging from two or three GCSEs, grade C upwards.

Bearing this in mind, think first about how these results and your profile match your attainments and experience. Do they reflect the results and qualifications you have already obtained? Are the strengths and weaknesses as you expected?

These types of test can have drawbacks. Timing has to be accurate and variations in your timing can affect your scores. Similarly, if you are timing yourself and spent a disproportionate amount of time watching the clock to make sure that you stopped on time you may not have done yourself justice.

Your test score may also vary slightly if you are feeling particularly tired or a little panicky. And, finally, this type of test does tend to penalize the slow but accurate worker who checks answers as he or she progresses. This is because no account is taken of the number of correct answers versus the number of incorrect ones.

Level of results

When you look at the overall level of the results you should be able to compare it with your results in examinations and other tests.

If your results are generally below average, you are unlikely to do well in examinations, particularly against the clock. You may well find that practical subjects suit you better.

If your results are generally around the average, you probably did quite well at school but may not have taken many further qualifications of an academic nature.

If your results are generally above average, you are likely to do well in most areas and you may well be thinking of careers which involve further study and qualifications.

The level of your results gives you an indication of the ease with which you can tackle problems in these areas. A very determined and conscientious individual can sometimes achieve more than the results suggest. Similarly, a less well-disciplined individual may under-achieve generally. However, the level of your results on these tests should be roughly in line with your experience. If there is virtually no connection between the two, you may well be the one person in a thousand for whom these tests to not completely work and you would be wise to seek advice from a professional careers counsellor.

Pattern of results

There are two broad types of test and you should look first at the distinction between the two.

If you have done better on the verbal, numerical, perceptual and analytical tests you are likely to be more academically biased and will generally do well in areas where theoretical knowledge and an ability to 'see' the underlying structure are most valuable. These areas include professional jobs such as librarian, accountant or research scientist.

If, on the other hand, you did better on the technical, spacial and acuity tests you are more likely to do well in areas which primarily use 'applied' knowledge, such as engineering, applied sciences, and areas of management which rely on ability and experience.

For many people, however, there is no clear distinction between these two broad groups and you will need to look further at the interpretations.

There are many possible results but we will concentrate on the nine individual strengths and the many important paired combinations.

Look at your strongest score(s) to find out which profile is most representative of your underlying abilities.

Individual strengths

Verbal reasoning

This strength is the ability to reason with words. This is often connected with literary careers but is also a very important attribute in those careers which involve the ability to find the right word at the right time. This may be the spoken word or the written word and is the single most useful strength in any kind of academic study.

This strength is most noticeable in a career as an author, a copywriter, a poet, a salesperson, a teacher, a linguist or a personnel director.

Numerical reasoning

This ability is similar to, but not the same as, mathematical ability. It is the ability to 'think' in numbers rather than the ability to manipulate them. There are comparatively few careers which require numerical ability alone; it is more often mixed with other abilities. Careers which are heavily dependent upon this ability include those as an auditor, a wage clerk, or a bank teller. Many areas of finance depend on it too.

Perceptual reasoning

This ability requires you to 'see' abstract information and to make sense of it. It is one of the cornerstones of scientific thinking. The stages of building concepts, discovery and proving theories all rely heavily on this aptitude. Thus it is a key to most scientific-based careers, including those as a research scientist, a laboratory technician, a veterinary surgeon, a dietician, a hospital technician and similar science-based personnel at all levels.

Complex reasoning

This test is different from the other reasoning tests because, while it requires high intelligence, it does not always predict academic attainment in the same way that the verbal, numerical and perceptual tests do. It is often the case that people with no formal qualifications to speak of, yet who can do this test, achieve at a high level simply because they have the ability to work through the information contained in a problem. The test demands both a logical and a practical approach. This type of aptitude is often found in detective work, and it appears in politicians and in leaders of business who possess this underlying talent.

Spatial ability

This is the ability which enables you to visualize a solid three-dimensional object when given limited two-dimensional information. It is the cornerstone of understanding technical drawings, layout and the relationships between objects in space and as such it will be used heavily by draughtsmen, creative artists, hairdressers, photographers and designers.

Technical ability

This test reveals the naturalness with which you cope with the world around you. It has more to do with your basic reaction to a practical problem than your learnt response. You do not have to be 'practical' but you probably will be if you score highly on this test. It is of particular use in careers for mechanics, lathe operators, maintenance personnel and assembly workers. It is also one of the most important abilities in the range of skills needed by engineers.

Acuity skills

This is the ability to do routine tasks quickly and with great accuracy. It is one of the few aptitudes that can increase noticeably with practice but the results will give a realistic guide as to how 'easy' you find this kind of task compared with others.

It is of particular use in many clerical areas such as filing, typing and computer operating. It is also of importance in areas such as quality inspection.

Coding

This is a skill that is subtly different from the more typical type of administrative skills measured in the acuity section, although it is often the case that people who are good at checking words and numbers are also good coders. This is because the same disciplines of precision and attention to detail are required. At the same time, the ability to code using symbols is also quite distinct from other skills. For example, a good computer programmer may be hopeless at filing! This type of talent is mostly found in careers related to systems engineering, Web design and programming.

Analytical ability

This is the ability to make logical, factual connections and to impose a structure on what sometimes appears to be chaotic information. It reflects the ability to think quickly, confining yourself to the facts only, to solve problems and to deal with new ideas.

It is frequently combined with other aptitudes to indicate the direction in which this ability to think is going to be used. The particular test in this book asks verbal questions as this is the most common way in which this ability is actually used at work. Reasonable verbal ability is required as well as 'pure' analytical ability.

It is of particular importance in careers such as computer programmer, researcher or analyst.

Two main factor combinations

It is quite unusual to have one single strong ability and indeed, as can be seen from the examples, there are comparatively few careers which require just one. It is better to look at the major abilities and see where combinations of these could lead.

Verbal/Numerical   Here the ability to reason equally well in words and numbers is the key for careers which would include commercial managers, senior administrators, insurance agents and head teachers.

Verbal/Perceptual   A descriptive scientist is the most helpful single description here but the ability is also found in areas of science which are not quite so heavily dependent on numerical ability. For instance, biologists and geographers would have this combination together with authors of scientific books and scientific journalists.

Verbal/Complex   This combination describes an incisive, enquiring mind that manifests itself in precise communication. People with this talent are usually persuasive because they present their views so precisely, describing the issues logically and using exactly the right words to state their case. Careers could be in legal work, but in many other areas such as teaching, management and in the media.

Verbal/Spatial   This combination contains both the ability to use words and the ability to see three-dimensionally. This could be most useful for photojournalists, editors, creative directors, design consultants and publishers.

Verbal/Technical   This area is similar to verbal/perceptual but bases understanding on the technical or applied side of science rather than the more theoretical issues, hence technical writers, engineering representatives and patents agents would find this combination valuable.

Verbal/Acuity   This is the area where you are primarily dealing with words and having to do so with great accuracy and speed. Many 'office'-type tasks fall into this category and in particular those of legal executives, word processor operators, translators, proof readers, personnel assistants and secretaries would all be expected to have this combination as a strength.

Verbal/Coding   These talents may be found among people whose work is often specialized, involving research or the patient compilation of data. Careers are often 'behind the scenes'. The preparation of documents, interpretation of information and ordering of documents could be some of the works tasks involved. Careers could be in the legal and administrative areas, but also in other areas such as historical research, archives and organizational planning.

Verbal/Analytical   This combination is frequently found in people working at the professional end of a scale where the ability to understand what lies beneath the surface as well as the ability to describe it are needed. In particular, barristers, science journal editors, psychologists, philosophers and management consultants frequently have these strengths.

Numerical/Perceptual   These strengths are particularly valuable for the 'harder' scientific approaches, especially at the higher levels. Examples in this area would include analytical chemists, metallurgists, astronomers, nuclear physicists.

Numerical/Complex   This combination of investigative and numerical potential suits careers where the wider importance of numbers is important, for example, in the strategy of running a business and determining policy. It is not necessarily an ability with finance, though often people with this combination will reach the highest levels in an organization as a financial director, for example, but can be seen in certain financial functions, such as purchasing. Other areas might involve statistics and many areas of mathematics.

Numerical/Spatial   This is a comparatively unusual combination which links the ability to visualize with a 'feel' for numbers. Examples of suitable careers, however, would include surveying, architecture and art dealing.

Numerical/Technical   This is a common combination in the applied science and technical fields. Design engineers, physicists, tool makers and structural engineers need this combination.

Numerical/Acuity   The dual strengths are most valuable in many areas of finance. Insurance actuaries, accounts clerks, statisticians (producers) and information technologists (producers of information) need these strengths.

Numerical/Coding   This combination shows talent for applying numerical information in practical ways. Logic and accuracy, which are denoted by this pairing, will find an obvious outlet in careers where data has to be ordered systematically and meaningfully. Applications will be within information technology and also where financial information connects with systems work as in programming and analysis.

Numerical/Analytical   The emphasis changes slightly on to the underlying understanding of the numerical activities and the ability to describe these processes and is best illustrated by careers such as a statistician (analyst), stock broker, mathematician, systems analyst, information technologist (analytical) and psychometrician.

Perceptual/Complex   This combination reveals highly objective and logical powers. Careers may relate to areas of engineering, research, but also less obvious areas of work where an investigative type of intelligence is essential, including police investigation work itself.

Perceptual/Spatial   This is a slightly unusual mixture combining scientific understanding with the ability to visualize in three dimensions and is probably best identified by careers such as medical photography, biological illustration and radiography.

Perceptual/Technical   This is the combination that provides both an understanding of the scientific principle together with the application of the technical. It is found in many areas of technology but a few slightly more unusual ones would include careers as a hospital physicist, laboratory technician, heating and ventilation technician and inventor.

Perceptual/Acuity   Activities combining these two particular strengths are more specialist, requiring an understanding in science (particularly the softer sciences) and greater attention to detail. Careers such as pharmacy technician, pathology technician and medical administrator could be included here.

Perceptual/Analytical   This is really a very general combination which includes virtually all academic scientists and areas where the emphasis is on the underlying reasoning and the understanding of that reasoning, and the communication of that understanding, rather than necessarily having to apply it in a particular direction.

Complex/Spatial   This combination reveals talent for seeing how various parts of things lock and fit together. The 'things' or applications are very wide indeed due to the fact that this type of intelligence is able to 'see bits of puzzles in new ways'. It is sometimes in design, engineering, but also in relation to work touching human affairs this combination may be useful. However, people with these distinct aptitudes usually start out by obtaining some logical, objective qualification.

Complex/Technical   This shows practical and technical understanding. Even if you do not have the hand/eye coordination to repair machines and other things that go wrong, you are quickly able to see the cause of difficulties. However, practical talents often go beyond technology and may well involve the 'technology of human affairs'. So, people with this type of talent are often found as managers in some kind of operational or manufacturing setting.

Complex/Acuity   This combination suggests potential for dealing with the management of administrative issues. For example, careers might include office management within a wide range of organizational settings.

Complex/Coding   Strong abstract reasoning and exact ordering of information are required in many types of work connected with systems analysis and work connected with Web sites.

Complex/Analytical   Broadly, this combination reveals an intellectual potential that is able to make sense of what is under the apparent surface of information. You will be able to 'spot clues' quickly, so are useful when dealing with ambiguous information. Careers might be in legal work, politics, management and many other areas where communication is involved.

Spatial/Technical   Careers here would include electronics engineering, lithographic printing, technical illustration and orthodontics.

Spatial/Acuity   In this combination the visual ability together with an 'eye' for detail would benefit map tracers, print makers, animators and tilers.

Spatial/Analytical   A fairly unusual combination of abilities linking the visual with the more 'academic' approach but careers in this area could include art history, graphic programme design and economics.

Technical/Acuity   There are many 'technician' posts requiring great accuracy that would normally fall in this category. Some of the slightly more unusual ones are photographic technician, patents examiner, architectural draughtsman and undertaker.

Technical/Analytical   This is the combination that produces process engineers, material scientists, information technologists (technical) and quality controllers. It combines the ability to understand what happens with the ability to provide the abstract logic of why it happens.

Acuity/Analytical   This is a most unusual combination and mixes the ability to analyse and to think logically with an attention to detail normally found in the more clerical tasks. Some examples of the combination, however, would be marketing analyst, compensation and benefits adviser, historian. Together they also provide the kind of discipline often needed in academic research – particularly until one 'qualifies'!

Coding/Analytical   Detailed research and preparation of information are talents to be used in a career suggested by this combination. Historical research and similar research work would be possibilities, as would legal work, and many forms of editing and publishing.

There are, of course, other combinations of three or more strengths and these would need to be looked at carefully. By doing a little of your own combining and by using the Career Index in Chapter 6 it is possible to find a career which tends to suit your abilities best.

We must emphasize, however, that abilities are not all. You do need to be both interested in, and the kind of person who will fit best in, the kind of environment in which the particular type of job takes place. Your abilities are only one small part of your overall suitability for a career.

It is now time to move on to look at personality and motivation and to understand what indications they can give you of your most suitable natural career choice.

If you have abilities at a fairly even level, it is most important that you pay particular attention to personality and motivation. You are not a specialist and require a career with variety. What will make the difference between a routine job and a successful career for you will be how well the aspects other than ability suit you.

What are my hidden strengths? – My personality

You need to understand your personality if you are to be happy at work. It is fashionable at the moment for employers to equate happiness at work with effectiveness. It makes sense: if you are discontented you are unlikely to do your best work. You may even find yourself unwell for no apparent reason! Employers want people who are suited to the job.

This has not always been so. For example, the Victorian factory owner did not have to pay as much attention to the feelings of his workers as do today's employers. Where there is ample labour and a willingness to work because work is seen as a way to escape from hardship, employers are simply looking for 'pairs of hands' or technical skills. But as our idea of what we mean by 'produce' moves into careers where personal flair, originality and interpersonal skills are demanded, the picture changes.

We often use words such as lively, exuberant or cheerful to describe personality. Increasingly, work which does not require 'personality' is replaced by machines. But many jobs which appear monotonous or routine are still undertaken by people because of the particular skills required. These may be tasks on a production line where experience of assessing defects in quality goods is essential (cars are still 'eyeballed' before being sent to the showroom). Divers as well as astronauts have to contend with long periods of boredom and routine in conditions where movement and expression are obviously seriously restricted. In these and other highly skilled jobs, a particular kind of personality is required and employers have learnt to select people who can endure calmly and remain alert in particular conditions.

So it is essential that your personality should be taken into account. The happier you are at work the better it is likely to be for you, first because you will feel that you are achieving and second, for the business or industry you are in because, frankly, you are likely to contribute more. Additionally, labour is an expensive resource these days, and your employer will have less cost associated with rehiring, retraining, strikes, stoppage or wastage if you are happy.

There are lots of theories as to what personality consists of. Some words associated with personality which have passed into common usage, eg 'id', 'super-ego', 'libido', are not very useful when it comes to the practicalities of different types of work.

You may well ask whether it is worth measuring personality. The question is often asked more directly: Is personality measurable? Our personality as it expresses itself in moods and other behaviour is infinitely variable; we all seem to have the potential at different times to be able to take on different types of personality. Sometimes we are not even acting; we become angry or obstinate or emotional or generous or frightened or quiet or noisy even though we do not normally act in this way. It is almost as though we can change ourselves, like a chameleon, to fit the conditions or the demands that are placed upon us.

It is our experience that most of us can act 'out of character' for a short time. We might 'go along with' situations in which we are unhappy, or even dislike, for the sake of convenience. But our 'normal' personality always seems to reassert itself.

This is not to say that we do not ever change. We change as a result of experience and through self-awareness. Shyness has been shown by researchers to change sometimes considerably as a person gets older. Personality changes can also come about through self-awareness or self-assurance, simply through a decision to change an aspect of yourself. People often do this by working hard to change something about themselves they do not like. You don't like public speaking? Take a public speaking course and keep on practising and you will find that it becomes second nature. You feel left out at parties? Rehearse a number of jokes before you go to your next party and you will find that you are becoming the life and soul. Afraid of strangers? An analyst or counsellor will be able to help you find out why this is 'blocking' your personality. To discover how to unblock your personality, read *Total Leadership*, also published by Kogan Page.

What, then, is your 'normal' personality? There is no doubt that you have a personality which is recognizable and familiar to the people who know you. You behave and react in characteristic ways. This is why people make relationships with you; it is why you are recognized by old friends and renew friendships even after many years in which you may have gone a completely different way from someone you grew up with. People say, 'You haven't changed a bit'.

It is because people have identifiable and consistent personality characteristics that it is sensible to relate these to a job. But bear in mind that as your own personality grows and changes you may need a career which does not stifle you. Some careers are like cul-de-sacs: they can be very comfortable and rewarding if they are going to suit you all your working life, but they can become a trap if you would prefer to be working along a different career path.

For example, your personality attributes of factual-mindedness may have led you to pass examinations and obtain a career as a technical expert – perhaps you are now a technician or scientist, or maybe you have become a statistician or computer engineer. But then you become aware that you are not getting the opportunities you would like to meet other people in your work. You may decide you have some leadership qualities and want to get into some form of management. Are there opportunities in the career you have chosen at the outset to broaden yourself and to find new challenges or will you have to start all over again? Although many people nowadays do take up second careers, and no doubt this book will be of help to such people, it is often a painful and difficult reorientation. We would prefer your career to flow naturally onwards and upwards rather than be filled with starts, stops and reversals.

Are you still unsure about the importance of personality upon career? You won't mind then if the surgeon has a 'flip', cheery or casual approach as he picks up his scalpel! Nor will you mind, as you board your plane taking you to your holiday in Majorca, that the technician fixing the engine is 'laid back'. And if you are an employer you will see no disadvantage in taking on as salespeople those who are either grouchy or too afraid to say boo to a goose. In our work connected with vocational guidance we have met thousands of people with whom we have discussed careers and we have become increasingly convinced of the folly of pursuing a career which is inconsistent with a person's type of personality. Too often we have seen people strive to achieve something for which they did not have the necessary characteristics and then feel a failure as a result. This is unnecessary. It is much better to enjoy doing what suits you. Here again, a little self-awareness helps. Stubbornness and determination can be excellent qualities and will help you achieve a task but taken too far these same qualities can turn into obstinacy and foolhardiness. It is far more sensible, if you find a career stressful, to lick your wounds and try something that suits you better. You should not stick at it just for the money or because you are trying to prove something to yourself.

Whatever your age now, your personality will have some stabilized traits and it is these that we can apply to different kinds of work. However, you need to bear in mind that your personality may appear to grow or change as you become more aware of your potential. Even doing the personality questionnaire can help you to increase your self-awareness so that you may well see yourself differently from the person you were before! But don't expect to change very radically or quickly and don't go into a career which manifestly does not fit your characteristics simply because you admire people who are different from yourself.

Will the personality test tell you anything you do not already know about yourself? Probably not; but there is little doubt that you know yourself better than anybody else does. At the same time you may not know how to relate your personality to different jobs. The personality test will help you to structure your ideas about your personality in useful ways. It will not measure all of your personality and it is not intended to deal with those aspects which are more relevant to your personal and private life. Here we are concerned with how your personality relates you to one type of work rather than another. Nobody has a multi-potential personality and just as personality enables us to achieve in some ways, it limits what we may achieve in others.

Let us take the case of the sales personality which most people would agree has distinct characteristics. These are in contrast to many of the characteristics required in other careers such as, for example, that of scientific researcher. For the salesperson interpersonal skills come first and foremost, with technical abilities usually a secondary requirement. It is the reverse for the researcher: where acquired skill and knowledge characterize the jobs, technical ability is vital. Here, paradoxically, a strange phenomenon may occur: salespeople often admire education and wish they had a quieter, more academic disposition; conversely researchers sometimes feel that career development is inhibited, not by exam prowess, but by lack of a more sociable and confident nature. Obviously this is not always the case, but we have witnessed it often enough to know that a great many people admire characteristics in others that they do not have themselves. However, it is wise to concentrate on those continuing aspects of our personality, however much we might want to change ourselves. Not to do so is as profitless as trying to walk through a low doorway without bending one's head or, not being a swimmer, diving straight into the deep end!

The personality tests

It is easier to spot what ability tests are trying to get at than it is with the tests of personality. In fact you may feel that the personality tests are trying to catch you out. This is not really the case! If you try to second guess the question or reply in a way that you know is not true for you the only person you will be catching out is yourself. The aim is for you to see certain aspects of your personality as clearly as possible. You can then relate the way your personality typically expresses itself to different types of work.

As you take these tests it may seem to you that you are answering one way now but might feel differently tomorrow and therefore respond in a completely different way. Feelings do change from day to day but they are not likely to change sufficiently to alter the results significantly.

When you respond to the personality tests it is best to think of yourself as you are now. Do not pretend that you are somebody else and do not think of yourself as you would like to be or think perhaps you could be. As a matter of fact, nearly everybody thinks that there is a better person within them trying to get out and that if only they were given the right chance then that person would emerge. In fact it is true, because no one is ever likely to be completely self-satisfied and therefore we are all trying to change ourselves in small ways. Even though the intent of these tests is to discover the real you, it is going to be most useful if you respond to the tests in a way that is a true statement about you, your feelings and your behaviour. In this way we will be able to draw some practical conclusions.

If you really are in two minds as to how you should take a test then it is probably best to take it twice. First of all take it as you feel you actually are now and see how your results come out. Then take it again, bearing in mind the personality characteristics you truly believe you would like to have. You will then be able to see whether you would really like the type of work done by people with the characteristics you admire. You can do this for interest rather than for any practical purpose. However, if you are confused at the end of all the tests about whether you have the personality to take on the career which appeals to you or whether you can change your personality in ways that you think you would like, then you had better see a vocational guidance counsellor.

Instructions

In all the personality tests you are asked to say whether you agree or disagree with various statements. Remember that there are no right or wrong answers. The answers you give will reflect your general thoughts and feelings. It is often difficult to say clearly whether you agree or not but just put down what tends to be true for you.

In completing the personality tests do not think about careers at all. Just think about yourself and your behaviour in all aspects of your life. You should circle the answer which agrees with the way you normally feel. Although it is difficult to be absolutely certain about some of the statements, do not spend too long making up your mind. It is generally just as good to give a quick response as to spend a long time mulling over the possibilities.

Do not leave any questions unanswered. The example below has been done for you.

Example:
When I sleep I very rarely dream   I   **YES**   (NO)   G

If you circle NO, this indicates that you do in fact dream.

Ignore the letters on each side of YES and NO: these will be explained later. Now carry on with Part 1 of the questionnaire.

The personality questionnaire

Part 1

1. I generally like to work by
   myself in my own way   I   YES   NO   G

2. I quickly get to know new
   people   A   YES   NO   P

3. Little mistakes I have made
   sometimes worry me   E   YES   NO   F

4. I often do things without
   thinking   L   YES   NO   C

5. I cannot forget my problems
   very easily   E   YES   NO   F

6. I have no difficulty in settling
   down to work on something
   difficult   C   YES   NO   L

7. Even if everyone else disagrees
   I say what I think   A   YES   NO   P

8. I prefer someone else to be
   the leader   P   YES   NO   A

9. I like to do the same thing
   as my friends   G   YES   NO   I

10. I try hard to make sure I do not
    hurt another person's feelings   E   YES   NO   F

11. I like to do a thing carefully to
    make sure it is done correctly
    even if it means giving up
    something else   C   YES   NO   L

12. Many things I read about in
    books and newspapers are sad   E   YES   NO   F

13. I frequently find it difficult to
    admit that I may be wrong   F   YES   NO   E

14. I usually take life as it comes	C	**YES**	**NO**	L
15. I think I work best in a team	G	**YES**	**NO**	I
16. I prefer to be at home rather than go to parties	P	**YES**	**NO**	A
17. I am always interested in the latest fashions	L	**YES**	**NO**	C
18. There is too much pain and misery in this world	E	**YES**	**NO**	F
19. I hate to be sitting down for too long	L	**YES**	**NO**	C
20. I am quick to try exciting new things	L	**YES**	**NO**	C
21. I am confident in most situations	F	**YES**	**NO**	E
22. I do not get as easily upset by things as other people	F	**YES**	**NO**	E
23. I support my friends no matter what	G	**YES**	**NO**	I
24. I sometimes worry about what others think of me	P	**YES**	**NO**	A
25. I nearly always have something to say in a discussion	A	**YES**	**NO**	P
26. I sometimes lie awake thinking about little things that have not gone quite right	E	**YES**	**NO**	F
27. I do not mind telling others about my private feelings	G	**YES**	**NO**	I
28. I do not know what I would do without my friends	G	**YES**	**NO**	I
29. I often do things without informing others	I	**YES**	**NO**	G

30. I like to win people round to my way of thinking	A	YES	NO	P
31. I often get sidetracked while doing something	L	YES	NO	C
32. After I have made a decision I am likely to change my mind	L	YES	NO	C
33. I like to help people get to know each other	A	YES	NO	P
34. The fun of having a secret is being able to pass it on	G	YES	NO	I
35. I find it difficult to make a decision if it is going to upset someone	E	YES	NO	F
36. I prefer to listen than to talk	R	YES	NO	A
37. I soon make it up after an argument	A	YES	NO	P
38. I am more or less happy with myself as I am	C	YES	NO	L
39. I like people to ask me before borrowing my things	I	YES	NO	G
40. I like to share my problems with my friends	G	YES	NO	I

Part 2

In Part 2 of the questionnaire you have to think about how others might describe you. In doing this, try not to be either modest or immodest: your answers should reflect truthfully notions of the feelings you suspect that others have of you. (If you ask these questions directly of friends or family, make sure you get a truthful and not a diplomatic answer and ask yourself also how biased those people might be.)

Part 2 consists of a list of words or phrases which people may use to describe you. You are to ask yourself whether people in general would use this word or phrase to describe you. Again, you are asked to circle one of the answers – **YES** or **NO** – as you did in Part 1. Again, take no notice of the letters at this stage; their purpose will be explained later. Now complete Part 2 of the personality questionnaire.

People would generally describe me as:

1. Company-seeking	G	**YES**	**NO**	I
2. Self-determining	I	**YES**	**NO**	G
3. Relaxed	C	**YES**	**NO**	L
4. Ostentatious	A	**YES**	**NO**	P
5. Retiring	P	**YES**	**NO**	A
6. Sentimental	E	**YES**	**NO**	F
7. Conforming	G	**YES**	**NO**	I
8. Confident	A	**YES**	**NO**	P
9. Impatient	L	**YES**	**NO**	C
10. Animated	L	**YES**	**NO**	C
11. Hearty	A	**YES**	**NO**	P
12. A dissenter	I	**YES**	**NO**	G
13. One of the crowd	G	**YES**	**NO**	I
14. Sensitive	E	**YES**	**NO**	F
15. Willing to accept others' advice	G	**YES**	**NO**	I
16. Effusive	A	**YES**	**NO**	P
17. Shy	P	**YES**	**NO**	A
18. Influenced by friends	G	**YES**	**NO**	I
19. Realistic	F	**YES**	**NO**	E
20. Highly strung	L	**YES**	**NO**	C
21. Unfeeling	F	**YES**	**NO**	E
22. Overmodest	P	**YES**	**NO**	A

23. Impulsive	L	YES	NO	C
24. Soft-hearted	E	YES	NO	F
25. Shocking	L	YES	NO	C
26. Go your own way	I	YES	NO	G
27. Tranquil	C	YES	NO	L
28. Blunt	F	YES	NO	E
29. Dreamy	E	YES	NO	F
30. Moderate	C	YES	NO	L
31. Stand on your own feet	I	YES	NO	G
32. Factual	F	YES	NO	E
33. Bashful	P	YES	NO	A
34. Keeps 'open-house'	A	YES	NO	P
35. Unruffled	C	YES	NO	L
36. Thin-skinned	E	YES	NO	F
37. Placid	C	YES	NO	L
38. Objective	F	YES	NO	E
39. Nervous	P	YES	NO	A
40. A 'loner'	I	YES	NO	G

How to mark the test of personality (the FLAG test)

The letters beside the words 'yes' and 'no' were deliberately changed around and put in different columns in order to prevent you from perceiving what the test was getting at. Of course, you can quickly 'see through' the test if you want to because it is hard not to be conscious that the items seen related to each other in the same way. At the same time, mixing up the questions and changing the answers around in this way is likely to keep you thinking; it 'keeps you on your toes' and will therefore produce a truer assessment of your personality, which is what we want.

To mark the test, start with Part 1 and count up the number of times you have circled either 'yes' or 'no' by the letter F. This will give you an F score. Enter this in the table below. Do the same with the letters L, A and G.

Repeat this with Part 2. You can then add both parts for each four letters so that for each letter you get a total out of 20.

In order to check that you have added up your score correctly, take each letter in turn and add the score you have obtained for that letter to the number of times you circled the letter that goes with it. You can see that E goes with F, C goes with L, P goes with A and I goes with G. In each part the score for each pair of letters should make 10. The maximum score in Part 1 is 10 and in Part 2 is 10.

Each of your scores relates to a different aspect of personality. They can be dealt with as a whole and indeed they should be because your personality also acts with all its parts. However, for the purpose of understanding your personality it will be useful to look at the four aspects separately.

Personality test results

Part 1	+	Part 2	=	Total
F		F		
( )	+	( )	=	_____
10		10		20
L		L		
( )	+	( )	=	_____
10		10		20
A		A		
( )	+	( )	=	_____
10		10		20
G		G		
( )	+	( )	=	_____
10		10		20

Being a factual or feeling personality

You can be both factual and feeling in the way that these descriptions are used in everyday language but in this personality test these words have particular meanings; a person may like to work with factual information, for example, but still have feelings! Therefore it is important to understand what these words mean as far as the test is concerned.

The characteristics of F

The F scale gives you an idea of how much attention you pay to feelings and whether you will want to deal with them in a work situation. Many people think that dealing with feelings, which often involves understanding and consideration of other people's point of view, prevents a job from getting done. If you hold this view then feelings will be a distraction and you will want to get on and accomplish a task with the minimum possible fuss.

The higher your score on the F scale, the more likely it is that you have a realistic, down-to-earth, no-nonsense approach to life. You probably like to deal with factual problems which require a logical approach so that you 'know where you are'. You like to see issues as clear and outcomes as certainties. Probably you will not like vagaries and jobs which are incomplete; you like order and systems.

The positive aspect of the factual personality is the ability to boil down all sorts of issues in a clear way. Your objectivity allows you to get somewhere and make progress. You are practical and can achieve definite results. Keeping yourself detached allows you to be analytical and often perceptive.

The disadvantage of being factual is that you can have difficulty with issues of a more emotional kind which cannot be easily classified. You may as a result prefer to be in an environment where emotional issues do not 'contaminate' the problem that you are dealing with. Your austere and logical approach pays full attention to the intellectual, but at the expense of losing out on the emotional side of things. You may be able to see what is in front of you or understand with your mind but you will be less able to feel whether issues are right or wrong because they cannot be objectively demonstrated.

If you are high on the F scale you will probably be drawn towards careers in which you can work with facts, information, objects or equipment. You may like working with people but it is the end product or job itself which appeals to you.

The characteristics of E

If you have a low score on the F scale then you are tending much more towards being sensitive. You will be keenly aware of what is said to you and about you and the way things are said will grab your attention. You will probably feel far less involved with things than about people. Logic and order will appeal to you much less than expression.

If you are very low on the F scale you will often have the ability to see both sides of an argument. You will be able to see how important an emotional issue may be. Emotional reasons for making decisions will be of more value to you than objective or legal reasons.

The disadvantage of being sensitive to feelings is that you can sometimes respond too strongly to your sense of injustice. Do you take things too personally? If you do, you might slow other people down if they haven't realized what is bothering you. Maybe you are a bit dreamy and maybe you are impractical.

If you tend more towards the feeling end of the scale then you may well feel frustrated if your work gives you no opportunity to use your intuition. In common with people of an artistic bent you can sometimes feel discouraged or burdened by the feelings you have but out of the ferment can arise creative expression. This might find fulfilment within the arts themselves or an arts-related environment. Alternatively, you may find that your sensitivity does give you an understanding into other people's problems.

As a rough guide you can compare your own score on the F scale with those of other occupations. Remember that the examples given below also have three other aspects of personality which we are not dealing with here, so you may not be able to identify completely with any of the occupations. Nonetheless, you can ask yourself what characteristics you have which are like those found in the occupations below. Simply mark your own score with a cross on the scale.

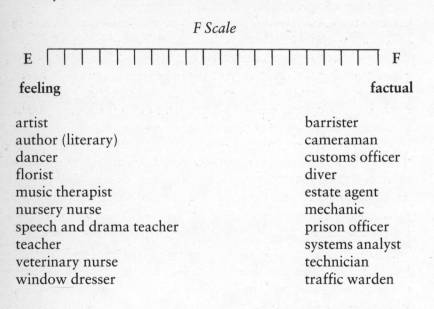

F Scale

E |||||||||||||||||||||| F

feeling   **factual**

artist	barrister
author (literary)	cameraman
dancer	customs officer
florist	diver
music therapist	estate agent
nursery nurse	mechanic
speech and drama teacher	prison officer
teacher	systems analyst
veterinary nurse	technician
window dresser	traffic warden

Being a calm or excitable personality

Whichever end of the scale you are you can get very frustrated in a job which does not correspond with this aspect of your temperament. If you are in the middle on the scale you might be able to 'bend' one way or the other to some extent, but it is difficult for you to act out of character for very long in a career which strongly requires one characteristic rather than the other.

The characteristics of L

The excitable person tends to react quickly to situations and to people. If you are like this, you will prefer things to be fast-moving; you enjoy change and variety. You may be spontaneous and make decisions 'off the top of your head'. If you are extreme, you will prefer to have many interests and you might have something of a 'butterfly mind'.

There are many positive aspects of being excitable. First, you can be very good company because you are amusing. You latch on to ideas quickly. You might almost be bubbly and effervescent. Your enthusiasm can be contagious. You want to get on and do things, and you will probably work best in a lively and frenetic career where everything is happening at once. Activities connected with the media and entertainment could interest you because of the constant variety.

A negative aspect of this personality is that you might find it difficult to finish something you have started. In fact, you sometimes have too many interests and fail to see things through to their conclusion. Because your interests are often superficial, people who are more serious or permanent might distrust you. You can also be a poor organizer. How many times are you late for appointments? In spite of this, you can probably avoid criticism through personal flair.

The characteristics of C

If you are on the lower end of the scale and are therefore of a calm temperament, you will probably have a consistent and dependable disposition. Do you ever get ruffled by anything? – Probably not. If you do, you probably wait for things to sort themselves out rather than interfere or make a scene.

The good thing about being calm is that you can act as a firm anchor when others begin to panic. You may often save the day because your unhurried and deliberate approach wins through. People will depend on you and admire you. For example, lots of men will smoke pipes in order to try to be like you! You will be good in a job where steadiness is required since you plan your work carefully and get it done properly as well as on time.

On the minus side, a certain amount of dullness may be attributed to you. This is unfair, of course, but you may have to admit that sometimes you are a bit predictable. Do you really have to weigh matters up so carefully? And at times you seem so self-assured as to be almost pompous or smug. However, we need you since without your steady hand on the tiller, where would we all be?

You can see that in some careers the work is carried out in an apparently immediate, impulsive and spontaneous way, and reactions have to be to the immediate subject of interest. There is sometimes a good deal of apparent pressure in such careers; this keeps people highly charged or keeps their adrenalin flowing. Alternatively, there are other careers much more suited to the placid and easy-going disposition.

Mark your own score with a cross on the L scale and see if you can identify with any of the careers which exemplify this characteristic. Bear in mind that in the examples given below other characteristics may also be required.

L Scale

C |||||||||||||||||||||| L

calm   **excitable**

administrator	advertising executive
ambulance crew	bar person
art therapist	conference executive
doctor	dancer
draughtsman	demonstrator
ergonomist	direct sales agent
firefighter	dresser
guard	hairdresser
librarian	marketing assistant
lighting technician	masseur/masseuse
osteopath	model

police officer

restorer

scientist

secretary

surgeon

theatre administrator

work study officer

public relations assistant

retail assistant

window dresser

Will I need to be aggressive to do well?

The answer to this question depends on what you mean by 'well': if you mean material success, the answer is probably yes. If you mean that you also want to have authority and influence over others, the answer is also likely to be yes. But the word 'well' can also have other meanings if you value contentment, peace of mind or co-operation rather than conflict. It will be obvious to you that some careers require a more 'pushy' approach than others. This scale is about how active and determined you are likely to be in going out into the world and getting what you want.

The characteristics of A

A person who is high on the A scale has an aggressive or bullish approach, and as many women can get high scores on this scale as men. Such characteristics are not generally associated with feminity: aggression has of course to do with dominance and Western society has hitherto assumed that women play a largely subordinate role. This need not necessarily be the case and attitudes towards the role of females are changing – probably because there is so much evidence around these days that women can be excellent leaders! Anthropologists have found plenty of evidence of female-dominated societies, so male dominance can in no way be regarded as an unchangeable biological characteristic.

The aggressive scale describes someone who is 'go-getting'. If you are like this, you will go out and get what you want rather than wait for it to come to you. You can be impatient at times. You will show confidence in yourself or at least such a strong need to achieve that you will overcome barriers.

You may think that the good aspect of having some aggression is that there has to be someone to organize others. You probably welcome change too. Others may look to you for leadership, recognizing your willingness to push ahead and perhaps even take risks. You are not easily put off and might be able to bluff your way out when you are in a tight corner. You may be able to make money or make things happen.

On the negative side, you will often hurt others' feelings. You charge forward so much that you can be like a bull in a china shop. You may not even realize the trail of misery and hurt feelings that you have left in your wake. Getting up and doing obviously has consequences for other people. However, you may feel that it is their own fault if they get in the way. You will find people easy to deal with even if you do have to manipulate them a bit or perhaps tell them only what they need to know. You will probably be drawn to careers which give you power and influence.

The characteristics of P

If you are of a passive disposition, you will have the ability to work in a structured way and pay attention to detail. You have a strong stoical streak and can put up with things when others would complain or rebel. You are good in the type of career in which you are behind the scenes. You will try hard to please and others will include you in their activities because they find your conscientiousness and reliability valuable.

The drawback of being too passive is that you may have difficulty in actually communicating your own needs to others. You put up with things because you fail to put yourself across. You will avoid making a fuss and of course if you resent being unappreciated it really is your own fault. However, you can get embarrassed so perhaps it is better to stay out of the limelight. You've got doubts about your self-confidence and you may not be able to step out of the boundaries of what others expect of you as well as the limits you have imposed upon yourself.

Mark your score with an X on the A scale below. Again, the careers listed below may give you an idea of those which would more or less suit you.

A Scale

P | | | | | | | | | | | | | | | | | | | | | A

passive   **aggressive**

bacteriologist	actor/actress
book-binder	bank manager
computer operator	beautician
dressmaker	broker
dietician	club manager
engraver	courier
gamekeeper	editor
gardener	entertainments officer
goldsmith	export salesperson
historian	fashion buyer
illustrator	hotel manager
library assistant	liberal studies teacher
lighthouse keeper	negotiator
patents examiner	publican
picture framer	public relations manager
potter	publisher
proof reader	reporter
storekeeper	speech and drama teacher
technical writer	transport manager

Should I work by myself?

People are important to you just as they are to everybody else. The often quoted statement 'No man is an island' is true. But some of us like to have more contact with people than others. There are various factors which determine whether we want to spend most of our time with people, and whether this should be with many people or just one or two. Some of us can only take people in small doses, feeling happier when we are working by ourselves, largely undisturbed. In some careers, the end product does not require much communication with others, for example if the work is highly specialized. But these are few and far between and some amount of social skill is present in almost every job. Whether you are going to be involved in management or as part of a work group or team, you will have to take some account of the necessity in most careers to associate with others.

The characteristics of G

If you are high on the G scale you like to go along with people and feel that you belong. Wanting to be with people has nothing to do with aggression or self-confidence. In fact, those who are very high on the G scale might well feel exposed on their own; they prefer to have others to turn to for assistance and advice. Such people often club together and are loyal to the team. They do not like to rock the boat, not because they are passive or sensitive but simply because they set a high value on team membership. At the other end of the scale is the independent-minded person who is inclined to make decisions alone rather than as part of a group. If you are low on the G scale you are not necessarily lacking in confidence but you prefer to be self-reliant. However, a low score often indicates some social shyness. Do you sometimes find it difficult to break the ice?

The advantage of being high on the G scale is that you are going to fit in extremely well. Your interest in people will literally cement a team together; you often bring out the best in people who will recognize and respond to this interest. Group loyalty and dependability are also useful characteristics, as is commitment to the team goals. You will do well in careers where interpersonal contact is necessary since you will relate to others quickly and easily.

On the negative side, the fact that you are a 'high G' personality implies some lack of individuality since you subordinate your own desires to some extent for the sake of the group. There may be some trade-off – such as originality for friendship. The very fact that you fit in can make you conventional and ordinary. Another issue which sometimes arises is that your fellow-feeling may prevent you from taking action which might offend others; the tendency to protect people you like may not be in the interests of the organization. In fact, it may not even help the other person in the longer term. For example, if you help to draw attention away from somebody who is not pulling his weight in an organization you may not be doing the best thing to help your friend face up to the difficulty. This kind of behaviour indicates that for you, the business exists for the benefit of the people who work in it rather than for any other reason – such as making a product or even a profit!

The characteristics of I

At the other end of the scale the independent-minded person makes decisions alone. If you are low on G, this does not necessarily imply that you dislike people (though you might very well do so). You certainly feel that, when it comes to achieving what you want, you are going to do much better under your own steam. You probably do not like social situations very much. Projecting yourself in a group is something you simply have to endure.

Positive aspects of being independent-minded are the many opportunities open to you. A high value is still put on self-reliance in many jobs, where you may be in the company of others but can largely shut yourself off when it comes to doing your actual work. The important thing is for you not to have to depend on others for the way your work turns out, to be able to use your initiative in your own way. You may be able to see the direct results of your own efforts.

The big disadvantage of being independent-minded is that you can sometimes do things off your own bat of which others may not approve. People do not know what you are up to and you can lose touch as well. You may be given some highly specialized role which makes you something of an outsider. Although you might enjoy this, you can also lose out because you will not know what is going on in the mainstream of things. And of course, you won't mind very much if you don't get any Christmas cards, will you?

The above comments talk about extremes on the scale as do the remarks related to all the other scales. Mark your F score on the scale below and see which careers you tend to identify with.

G Scale

I ⌐ | | | | | | | | | | | | | | | | | | | | | | ⌐ G

independent   **group member**

independent	group member
accident assessor	air hostess/steward
archaeologist	auctioneer
architect	cashier
barrister	club manager
book-binder	club secretary
bus conductor	community worker
buyer	entertainments officer
chiropodist	firefighter
courier	house parent
craftsperson	interviewer
dentist	masseur/masseuse
designer	play leader
engraver	publican
health visitor	public relations manager
interpreter	remedial teacher
literary agent	sailor

literary critic	salesperson
milkman	soldier
photographer	youth worker
printer	
proof reader	
publisher	
reporter	
shepherd	
silversmith	
train driver	
writer	

Looking at your total personality

Having examined your four individual traits in detail it is time to get the full picture. Transfer your individual scores to the FLAG graph on the next page, marking each appropriate place with an X as in the example.

Example:

	F	L	A	G	
High	20	20	20	20	High
	18	18	18	18	
	16	16	16	16	
	14	14	14	14	
	12	12	12	12	
	10	10	10	10	
	8	8	8	8	
	6	6	6	6	
	4	4	4	4	
	2	2	2	2	
Low	0	0	0	0	Low
	E	C	P	I	

Connect up your four scores. In the example, the results can be described as low, high, low, high (FLAG result: ELPG).

What should you do if your scores are in the middle or if some scores are relatively higher or lower? In these cases you must make your own judgement as to the tendency your FLAG test result shows. If your pattern is not absolutely clear, you may have to try out several of the combinations below which are close to your own results.

If you remain confused as to which FLAG description suits you best, you may have to do the test over again, trying to be more sharply aware of your personality as you do so. Alternatively, you may have a broad personality and be able to fit into many areas. For you, your aptitudes or your motivation is going to be more important in determining your career.

FLAG test result

	F	L	A	G	
High	20	20	20	20	*High*
	18	18	18	18	
	16	16	16	16	
	14	14	14	14	
	12	12	12	12	
	10	10	10	10	
	8	8	8	8	
	6	6	6	6	
	4	4	4	4	
	2	2	2	2	
Low	0	0	0	0	*Low*
	E	C	P	I	

My FLAG result is: _____

Types of personality

The sixteen major combinations below can be used as a means by which you can (a) understand yourself more clearly, and (b) relate your own personality to broad types of work.

FLAG	Character
1. FLAG	Politician
2. FLAI	Entrepreneur
3. FLPG	Helper/Assistant
4. FCAG	Manager
5. ELAG	Campaigner
6. FLPI	Free agent
7. FCPG	Provider
8. ECAG	Teacher
9. ELAI	Artist
10. FCAI	Advocate
11. ELPG	Helping hand
12. FCPI	Specialist
13. ELPI	Rolling stone
14. ECAI	Adviser
15. ECPG	Supporter
16. ECPI	Loner

1. The Politician (FLAG)

Your personality is predominantly factual, excitable, aggressive and group-orientated. Although you may not have all these characteristics in the extreme, their presence is likely to help you in negotiating, campaigning and initiating activities which others need persuading to follow. You are likely to be active, engaged in many tasks and with many contacts. A feature of your personality is the ability to switch interests, moving quickly from one subject to the next. You are never lost for an answer for long. You are energetic and don't get beaten down so that you eventually get what you want. Although you have lots of projects, you seem to be able to fit new ones in. Others are happy to give you responsibility and look to you as leader because you have ideas, confidence, practicality and interpersonal skills.

You may be 'in politics' as a politician proper or in some associated role; numerous careers afford opportunities which are not obviously political in the traditional sense. You may be working in some part of government service but could also be in business, having particular interests in organizational structure and corporate development.

Careers

advertising executive	politician and political agent
auctioneer	public relations director
club secretary	senior administrator
estate agent	sports coach/manager
managing director	

2. The Entrepreneur (FLAI)

Your personality is factual, excitable, aggressive and independent. You show determination in getting what you want, maybe at the expense of others. There is no doubt about it – you show a lot of drive and strength of purpose. You will have a buoyant and energetic personality. You can spot opportunities and also apply yourself selectively to make those opportunities work for you. It is unlikely that you will allow yourself to be held back by petty considerations. You will often go your own way and back your own judgement against others more conservative than yourself.

Your enterprising and self-reliant style is frequently found in business and in other activities connected with wealth generation. It is the independent-mindedness which, among your other characteristics, is the key to your success because you are prepared to act on your initiative; you will do what you want and wait for others to catch up with you. Typically, you will pursue activities in which you can do things your own way and set your personal stamp on things. You will also expect to see a measurable statement of your success. There are innumerable careers open to you.

Careers

agent (import/export)	property developer
buyer	publisher
marketing director	road manager
market trader	self-employed business person

3. The Assistant (FLPG)

You are factual, excitable, passive and group-orientated. On the one hand you have a down-to-earth, stable quality which makes you solid and dependable. At the same time you are a conformist and fit in with others well. This combination allows you to come to the fore in situations requiring personal skills, particularly those of tact and understanding. Your own resourcefulness is much sought after by others who appreciate your comforting and reassuring manner. You are likely to be popular as well as admired; you will know what to do in a crisis, keeping your cool while all about you others are losing theirs. You will enjoy challenges but you like to apply the skills you have learnt to overcome them. You find life interesting and enthusiasm rather than personal ambition is your main characteristic.

There are plenty of opportunities for you in all areas of work. In fact, your characteristics are so much in demand that you are unlikely to be out of a job. You fit well into the structure of many organizations and companies where your willingness and practicality are always appreciated.

Careers

air hostess/steward	masseur/masseuse
bar person	play leader
dental assistant	receptionist
hairdresser	secretary
house parent	

4. The Manager (FCAG)

You are factual, calm, aggressive and group-orientated. You are interested in people and have an excellent intuitive sense of what makes them tick. It will be of particular interest to you to be in charge of people in organizations where success can be judged by how well you achieve a task together. It is your aim to get things done with people and through people. Personally, you are organized and hard to ruffle. You enjoy planning ahead and marshalling your resources. You may distrust abstract or over-elaborate ideas, your own style being the product of experience and developed skills. You are likely to be methodical rather than inspiring, but at the same time, the fact that you don't take unmeasured risks means that you generally achieve what you want. Others feel confident in you and therefore you often find yourself in charge.

You will often 'keep things going' and make things work, particularly when people and materials are brought together. Ideally, you need to work in an organization of some kind. You want either to deal with products or equipment or to work towards some real goal where you feel you could achieve something tangible.

Careers

armed forces officer	production manager
bank manager	publican
general manager	retail manager
hotel manager	transport manager

5. The Campaigner (ELAG)

You are feeling, excitable, aggressive and group-orientated. These qualities mean that you are thoughtful towards people as well as full of ideas; you are aware and want to put things right. Your spontaneity and insight are admirable qualities. Put these together with interpersonal flair and you have someone who takes up causes. You are quick to spot injustice. All right, sometimes you may shoot your mouth off, but who cares – the point needed to be made! Your heart is in the right place, but you must be careful not to go off at a tangent. Your desire will be to do good, to make things better, to create a better world. You can be pushy and you may get emotionally involved: this is your strength, while your weakness is not knowing when to stop. However, people will often rely upon you to 'wield the cudgels' on their behalf.

You should look for careers in which people need a helping hand or someone to show them the way. You may supply the charisma and fortitude they lack. Be prepared for intense but short relationships at work as you move energetically and enthusiastically from project to project.

Careers

beautician	public relations executive
civil rights worker	speech and drama teacher
courier	teacher
demonstrator	union representative
journalist	

6. The Free Agent (FLPI)

You are factual, excitable, passive and independent. You can therefore work in your own way and at your own pace. But you are also able to fit in with others, even being willing to adapt your own schedule to fit in with theirs. You are able to 'go along with things' and you don't let things get you down. You enjoy having a skill and you enjoy the certainty of knowing what is expected of you. Relationships are on a basis of mutual respect. You probably have a boss, but may work unsupervised so that there is no one on your back.

You have the ability to apply your skills in new situations, but it is your skills and experience you rely upon as you are not a great risk-taker. Your self-reliance and liveliness are frequently misinterpreted as management potential. This may appeal to you at times, but it is not really what you want because it alters your relationships with people; you suddenly find yourself worrying about people and you prefer to be a free agent. Another thing to watch for is that you do not rely too much on a trade or skills which will become outmoded. Even so, you are very adaptable and hence very retrainable.

Careers

accounting technician	office machinery mechanic
bus conductor	painter and decorator
chef/cook	paramedic
chimney sweep	repairer
dietician	road patrol officer
interpreter	surgeon

7. The Provider (FCPG)

You are factual, calm, passive and group-orientated. While wanting to be with people, you have no desire to take charge; you want to fit in and usually do. You are not the type to ruffle others' feathers but will go along with the wishes of the majority. The stability and reassurance you present to the world make you accepted as a friend and as a trustworthy assistant. You do not get side-tracked by the irrelevant nor do you take on projects which are too large. In fact, you are reasonable in all things. You feel most comfortable where there is order and planning. Change is not your style – unless, that is, all the risks have been taken out.

You act as a constant, reliable force in keeping people together and your predictability and dependability make you a great team member. You are a mine of useful experience and information which others can rely upon. Preferred careers are likely to be in factual concerns, such as doing or making something practical. You will probably be actively involved in a team effort.

Careers

agricultural secretary	merchant sailor
ambulance crew	nurse

Armed Forces member	police officer
cashier	prison officer
firefighter	road gang worker
guard	

8. The Teacher (ECAG)

You are feeling, calm, aggressive and group-orientated. This combination of traits allows you to deal with an often demanding and hectic environment. But would you have it any other way? You are likely to be in tune with what is going on. In particular, you will pick up nuances in the behaviour of others. You will be quick to see ideas and possibilities. But you will also be consistent and firm. You will mix with others easily – and not just at work either, since you enjoy being responsible for others in your spare time as well. You will see another's point of view but you are also determined and have plenty of ideas of your own.

It is likely that you will have a definite skill or experience to offer. In fact, you are probably something of an expert. But it is unlikely to be the subject or content of your work which appeals to you so much as the opportunity to pass your knowledge and skill on to others. In many ways you are a leader, but due to your strong altruism and sensitivity you are rather more attracted to public service than diplomacy or business.

Careers

doctor	senior teacher
osteopath	social worker
psychologist	training officer
senior nursing officer	youth worker

9. The Artist (ELAI)

You are feeling, excitable, aggressive and independent. Ideas and expression are essential to you. You are often described as radical or impractical. In your search for novelty you can become uncomfortable and apparently at odds with the world. You are thoughtful and reflective, but have a sharp mind which quickly recognizes dissonance in many spheres. The need to survive can make you tough. At times you can have a defensive or prickly quality, owing to the strength of your feelings and principles. You can feel impassioned by both emotional and abstract matters. Thus, you vent your feelings in your art while you may harangue others about politics and the state of the world. It is unlikely that you mix much though relationships are probably intense, even stormy. With you, both socially and personally, it is all or nothing.

You need to work largely by yourself as you soon feel bored in a group; you have some unique idea and you need to work on it in your own way. Communication with others is most successful when you can present to them – in other words, when you make a 'statement'. What you create may be larger than life or it may be a distillation. The ordinary everyday world is unsatisfactory; you will take it and abstract the epitome and quintessential. As you can be both entertaining and challenging you will find opportunities in activities which others find diverting and thought-provoking.

Careers

architect	interior designer
artist	musician
author	sculptor
dancer	

10. The Advocate (FCAI)

You are factual, calm, aggressive and independent. These qualities make you formidable. The facts are at your disposal, you are clear about them and you can present them calmly and logically. There is no question of intuition. You will keep ideas and information to yourself. You will find yourself happiest in debate or at least in the presence of similarly sharp minds uncorrupted by sentimentality or lack of training. In fact, you set a lot of store by your own mind which you have, with some pride, honed to a sharp point. Essentially, you are self-reliant. People need you to sort out their problems, but relationships will be businesslike as opposed to friendly. It is the business or the point at issue that brings you together with others, rather than fellow-feeling.

You will do well in careers in which you need to keep your head, such as those situations where others get flustered, forget what they are saying, don't stick to the facts and take too much on trust. Your investigative and detached style is suited to careers where the objective truth needs to be ascertained and where there are legal or measurable issues to deal with.

Careers

barrister	police inspector
customs officer	solicitor
dentist	work study officer

11. The Helping Hand (ELPG)

You are feeling, excitable, passive and group-orientated. Others will find you interesting, responsive and want to be with you. Your main attribute is your willingness to try new things. You are eager and expressive. Lively situations appeal to you and you are happy when there's plenty going on; you are bored by routine and predictable situations. You probably hate figures and office work has very little appeal. As you are intuitive and creative you need an artistic environment, but you may lack the assertiveness and be too well disposed towards people to be a really successful artist in your own right. Second, then, is your need to associate with a team, to feel yourself part of a project. A group undertaking, where your own skills and personality complement those of others, will suit you best. You will never lack friends as you are such good fun to be with; your enthusiasm for life is infectious. At the same time, you may never settle at anything for very long because you tend to exchange stability for new opportunities.

Careers in which you find novelty as well as a group to identify with will suit you. You like to achieve quickly, so careers which require lots of study or preparation will not be so attractive.

Careers

chef/cook	receptionist
dresser	retail assistant
marketing assistant	stage-hand
nursery nurse	waiter/waitress

12. The Specialist (FCPI)

You are factual, calm, passive and independent. In other words, you have a clear, sharp and detached mind, uncluttered by the trivial or irrelevant. You are capable of applying yourself well to resolving problems. You are technically minded because you see issues logically. Typically, you work deductively: you are a glutton for knowledge and see the connections between apparently diverse bits of information. You fit in with people easily enough but will not socialize much because you 'have things to do'. Your life is well ordered and there are lots of things you want to get on with. You are frequently described as efficient. Others call upon you to help them solve problems, though not those of an intuitive nature. You appear to lack some of the human faults that so beset others and your 'pick yourself up and get on with it' attitude can be unnerving to those with less energy and self-reliance. Your usefulness arises from your organized approach and your expert background; your advice will be valuable because it is objective. However, it would be a mistake to believe that your technique and expertise could enable you to be a leader, because this requires a social sensibility which is not one of your strong points.

Careers

accounting technician	diver
actuary	driver

archivist	engineer
auditor	operational researcher
patents examiner	systems analyst
rating valuation officer	technician
referee	train driver

13. The Rolling Stone (ELPI)

You are feeling, excitable, passive and independent. If anything is important to you, it is not to get over-involved. Long and close contacts with people are particularly to be avoided. People should preferably stay at a distance: you do not make demands upon others and you would prefer it if they did not make demands upon you. Many things interest you but you will pursue few to a conclusion. You have a restless disposition that is hard to satisfy in the long term; you are not studious and tend to move on. On the other hand, you may have a wealth of scattered knowledge. The problem is to find a means of bringing it all together and applying it in some useful way. Unless you are careful, you may find yourself forever on the edge of things, flirting with people and with different activities. You are good fun in a social setting and when matters are light rather than serious you can be entertaining and even original.

What you achieve in your career may be determined largely by your early education; as you are not disciplined yourself, your early schooling may have led to success (and therefore entry qualifications) which you would not have obtained under your own steam. Generally, the work you do will depend upon luck and opportunity rather than your own fixed purpose in shaping your own destiny.

Careers

bar person	porter
dancer	production worker
disc jockey	shop assistant
entertainer	waiter/waitress
model	

14. The Adviser (ECAI)

You are feeling, calm, aggressive and independent. People as well as ideas fascinate you, but you may stay detached rather than becoming personally involved. You find the arts more appealing than technical subjects, but your steadiness makes you less of an artist than a commentator or critic. Again, the detached or logical element of your personality may lead to your shaping some world view of your own; you may have a philosophical bent. But rather than comment you like to get out and do – in other words, you like to test your theories in action. Although you work with people and may have an influential role, you remain essentially an outsider rather than insider. Nevertheless, you can establish contact easily and you have qualifications and experience as well as an authoritative manner.

You can sell your skills as some kind of consultant (though this may not be the actual title of your job). Part of your talent is your timing – knowing that others are ready to receive your initiatives. One drawback is that you can be too theoretical at times and this affects your relationships as well as the work itself. However, you are good value in 'pointing the way to go', in indicating how things ought to be in an ideal world.

Careers

analyst	librarian
business adviser/consultant	social scientist
human resources consultant	training officer
journalist	

15. The Supporter (ECPG)

You are feeling, calm, passive and group-orientated. You probably allow others to make the running. Indeed, it seems that you put yourself out for others. You certainly have insight and you have probably acquired useful skills which enable you to contribute very effectively to the well-being of others. Not only are you thoughtful and aware but you apply yourself consistently and calmly to making the most of your talents. You are a valuable addition to any team. You fit in easily and no one feels threatened by you. In fact, people like you a lot because they recognize that you like them and are prepared to care for them. They will unload their troubles on you and receive sympathy as well as skilled advice in return. You work well in a team where your skills complement those of others or where everybody's skills are the same. In this respect, you are essentially democratic and sharing. You enjoy being appreciated and valued and you resent being used or exploited. You have a strong inner motivation which makes you resist and back away if given orders.

You will find yourself in a career which demands insight, application and interpersonal skills. You are in many ways similar to the Helper but your skills are more on the human side rather than providing technical help.

Careers

counsellor	nursery teacher
hospital porter	remedial teacher
house parent	social worker
mental nurse	therapist

16. The Loner (ECPI)

You are feeling, calm, passive and independent. You want to work by yourself and are capable of doing so. It is not so much that you will forge ahead or leave others behind but a question of wanting to find a niche for yourself. Because you do not need much contact with people, you might read a lot or have other interests to occupy you. Characterized by intelligence, thoughtfulness and possibly even a gruff courtesy, you prefer to be detached. Shyness is a feature which may be misinterpreted as grumpiness or hostility: it is just your defensiveness and desire to remain in your own world. You are interested in many things, thoughtful and aware, but far-sighted rather than nearsighted. Although difficult to get to know, you can be intensely loyal. You have definite opinions and are slow to change.

Choose a career in which you can apply yourself in your own way and at your own pace. Although you may have plenty of contact with people, it is likely to be an incidental rather than a major feature of your work. Plenty of jobs give you the isolation and freedom you like. In most of them you will be working for an employer, unless you have an artistic skill which you can sell.

Careers

arborist	lighthouse keeper
curator	milkman
dressmaker	potter
farmworker	shepherd
gardener	thatcher
historian	

4

What do I enjoy? – My motivation

In some ways, motivation is even more important than ability or personality. You can probably think of examples of your own to support this view. How many people have you known with ability who have apparently just not bothered about achievement? Alternatively, you may also know and have certainly heard of people who have triumphed over all odds, who have 'made it' in something which they seemed completely unsuited for, who overcame disasters to win fame and fortune. What makes some of us go on when others give up? What makes some of us break out from our humble origins while others are trapped by their background? What is and is not possible for most of us is very largely determined by motivation.

The strength of the motivational factor is nowhere better exemplified than in the contrast between success in the 'real world' and educational/exam prowess. It is a strange fact that the educational system, with its selective approach to establishing academic excellence, is a poor predictor of success in later life. Thus, the School Dunce drops out at the earliest opportunity and becomes an Errand Boy, then a Trader, then a Merchant and finally a Businessman. He might employ business graduates and professional people to make even more money for him. Again, some intellectually able people fail to make the most of their potential because they lack the energy, drive or direction – all synonyms for motivation.

We can be motivated by many things: fear, love, envy, compassion. At a fundamental level, motivation arises from fears attached to deep and basic survival needs originating in our animal ancestry. Starvation is a powerful motivator! But once basic needs are satisfied, we begin to be motivated by activities which we enjoy for their own sake, not because they are necessary for our essential existence.

In most people's minds, a career comes mid-way between survival and enjoyment. Nowadays, is is not necessary for most of us to actually work in order to survive. Nobody is likely to starve to death. But if you want anything more than the basic essentials to keep you fed and sheltered then work will be important.

Is any kind of work going to be satisfactory and continually motivating? Are you prepared to trade your time and labour for a wage? Many people think in this way. What they are saying is in effect, 'I put up with my job because it provides me with the money to enjoy my leisure time.' This is an 'economic' view of work because it represents the exchange of labour for cash. It leads to the 'carrot and stick' principle of employment. As a philosophy it is far less popular with employees as well as employers than in the past. In an age where welfare benefits take the edge off the fear of destitution and tend in many cases to the provision of what 50 years ago would be called 'luxury' items, the idea of enjoyment at work as a motivator has arisen. It has become clear to employers that employees who enjoy doing their work are more productive than those who do not. It is no longer a case of wanting to work out of fear but wanting to work out of the satisfaction that the activity itself provides.

Your work will bring you various kinds of reward, but some of these will be intangible, such as contentment, satisfaction, respect, importance and affection. Fortunately, we are not all motivated by the same things and the opportunities open to us are diverse and innumerable.

At this stage in the book it will be clear to you that each of us is born with a unique intellectual structure and a unique personality structure, and of course we grow up in a unique situation. The influences upon us, particularly during childhood, prod and poke us in different directions. All the time we are testing out our hereditary potential against our environment. Sometimes we win, sometimes we lose (where winning can be defined as achieving that which makes us happy and losing as experiencing that which we find painful).

It is not always as clear cut as this since few of us are ever really free agents. In other words, not all of us have the same opportunities and many of us therefore feel blocked or curbed, never having been really able to try out all our talents or express ourselves fully. Maybe we encountered disapproval from adults. Maybe the courses we had to take at school never really suited us; we merely went along with what our parents expected. If we had known ourselves fully and known how to express ourselves in order to get what we wanted we would have gone in a different direction.

Nevertheless, most people have a pretty good chance as they grow up of finding out just what motivates them and what does not. What classes at school did you go to willingly or less willingly? What do you prefer to watch on TV? What do you do in your spare time? Is it maths or cookery? Do you prefer sport or reading? Do you like to go out with friends or watch television? In various ways, your motivation will have been 'shaped up'. There is a rich source of information all around you and you will have explored lots of possibilities, either directly as a participant or vicariously as an observer. You will have been mentally processing this information: picking it up, weighing, discarding, trying out, keeping or throwing it away.

Some things you like the sound of may not be immediately available but perhaps you are sufficiently motivated to get nearer to what you want. You may have to study in order to get even closer to the kind of activity which appeals to you. And all the time, through meeting people, reading, watching TV and so on you are making connections about how different careers interlock with certain kinds of aptitudes and personalities, and the different kinds of reward they provide. Consciously or subconsciously you will continually match yourself against the various possibilities. As you discover patterns in your own motivation and get to know yourself better, you will imprint this self-knowledge, figuratively speaking, upon the multitude of opportunities which present themselves. You will become aware that some of these patterns match better than others.

So how is it that with all this rich experience you still remain uncertain about what really motivates you? It may be that your interests have developed only on the basis of what has been available to you. Possibly you have already succeeded in something you were good at but feel you have other ideas to explore. Again, perhaps you have heard about lots of careers but find it difficult to know what they really involve. For example, you were a good swimmer at school but does this mean that you will enjoy being a diver? You were good at maths but what does becoming an economist entail? You started in the family business but never really felt fulfilled so would it be a good idea to return to study and, if so, what?

It could also be that your motivation has changed. Although this rarely happens quickly, it can do so over the years.

Finally, it is because many of us are motivated by a number of things which often seem in conflict with each other that we need to look carefully at the strength and direction of our motivation.

The motivation questionnaire allows you to look at your own personal motivation in a structured and practical way. It is designed to bring you down to earth. Stop dreaming, sort yourself out, get on and do it!

The motivation questionnaire

This is designed to investigate one important aspect of your motivation – that which is directed towards a career. The way the questionnaire works is to help you to make decisions about which among your interests is more or less important to you.

Although you may feel that you could develop new interests if you understood what was involved, your experience so far must be the starting point. However, the questionnaire often provides some surprising results. Perhaps because it can reveal and highlight possibilities in a systematic and meaningful way it can often bring into focus those areas of work which you perceive as giving you the most opportunity to express yourself – not only to obtain reward but also to find enjoyment and personal satisfaction in ways that only you can define.

The questionnaire is in two parts: it asks first what jobs and second what activities appeal to you. It is important for you to have some idea of the 'frame of mind' you are in as you take the questionnaire. Let us be clear about what this means. You could find yourself eliminating some of the alternatives because (a) you do not have the qualifications to do the job or (b) you do not think you could get the qualifications to do the job. Do not concern yourself with these issues; find out what appeals to you first, then let the ability tests assess whether you could do the job or not. In other words, if you do the questionnaire in a 'narrow' frame of mind, you might cut yourself off from some of the possibilities before you even start, because you will in effect by saying to yourself 'Oh, I couldn't do that (even though I might like to).'

Another frame of mind to avoid at this stage is one which is over-concerned with (c) pay or (d) status. There are many such considerations which could have a bearing upon your decision and it would be impossible to weigh them all in the balance; the best thing is to ignore them as far as you can. Simply ask yourself whether the occupation or activity appeals to you *in a general way*. It is the impression it makes on you which counts – you can evaluate your underlying reasons and the various circumstances which led you to make specific choices later. Remember, your results in the ability and personality tests will give you more concrete evidence of your suitability for a particular area of work than will your own opinion.

If you feel that it is impossible to divest your mind entirely of certain realistic and practical considerations, the best thing to do is to take the motivation questionnaire twice, putting yourself each time into a different frame of mind. You can then see how the results compare. For example, you might complete it 'realistically' the first time and the second time just 'let yourself go'.

Some of the choices you are forced to make in this questionnaire you will find will be easy; others will be difficult because both occupations will appear either equally dull or equally appealing. However, the questionnaire uses a 'forced choice' technique, which establishes a picture of the relative attractiveness of certain kinds of activity.

People sometimes object to choosing between two things they like equally or dislike equally. The forced choice compels you to make a decision. When you see that you do, on balance, prefer some types of activity to others, this information can be used to point to the specific careers that accord with your preferred interests.

There is no time limit to this questionnaire though you should not spend too long making choices. First impressions are generally as useful as decisions arrived at after much deliberation. Whether you work quickly or slowly through the questionnaire will not affect the result significantly.

Try to do each part of the motivation questionnaire without interruption. There is no reason why you should not have a break of whatever length you like between Parts 1 and 2. Both parts of the questionnaire are to be completed in the same way: you look at two occupations or two descriptions of an occupational activity and decide which one appeals to you more. It is a good idea to look up those careers which you do not know much about in order to see what they involve.

When choosing between the two careers or descriptions you have three points to award. If one occupation or description appeals to you more than the alternative you can give it three points and the other no points. If you are not sure, give the job you marginally prefer two points and the alternative one point. Give more points to the career or the description which has more appeal. You must always give away three points, no more, no less.

The points you have awarded should be written in the circles opposite the occupational titles or descriptions. In the first example, which has been done for you below, it is quite clear what sort of activity has the greater appeal.

Interpreter   ③

Gardener   ⓪

In the next example, the person has had more difficulty in deciding upon which activity he would rather undertake. On balance, he has decided to divide the points.

Manager of cinema   ①

Work with formulae and equations ②

Take no notice of the letters at the head of each column for the moment (the purpose of these will be explained later).

Now you are ready to take the motivation questionnaire.

The motivation questionnaire

Part 1

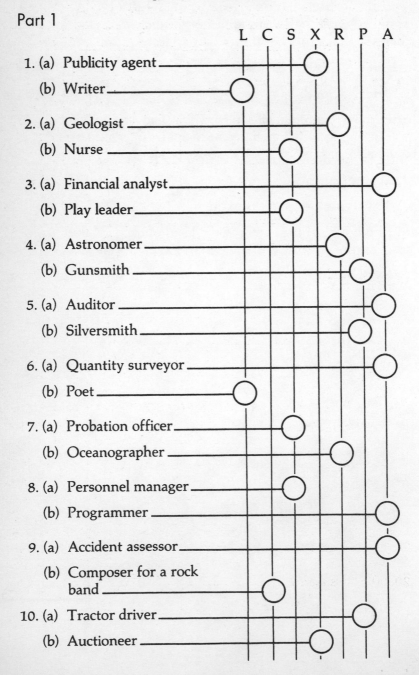

		L	C	S	X	R	P	A
1.	(a) Publicity agent				○			
	(b) Writer	○						
2.	(a) Geologist					○		
	(b) Nurse			○				
3.	(a) Financial analyst							○
	(b) Play leader			○				
4.	(a) Astronomer					○		
	(b) Gunsmith						○	
5.	(a) Auditor							○
	(b) Silversmith						○	
6.	(a) Quantity surveyor							○
	(b) Poet	○						
7.	(a) Probation officer		○					
	(b) Oceanographer				○			
8.	(a) Personnel manager			○				
	(b) Programmer							○
9.	(a) Accident assessor							○
	(b) Composer for a rock band		○					
10.	(a) Tractor driver						○	
	(b) Auctioneer				○			

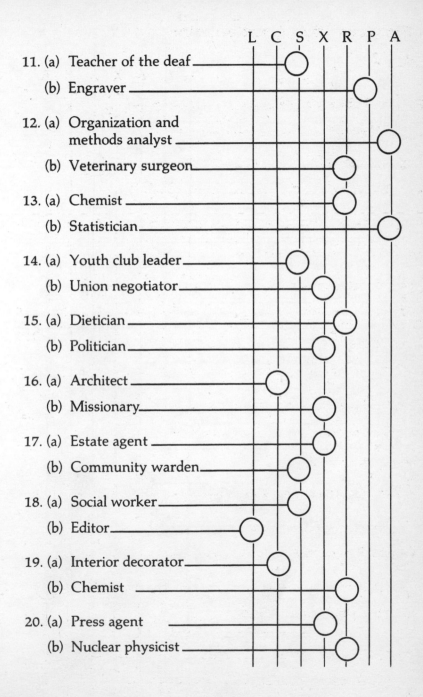

	L	C	S	X	R	P	A
11. (a) Teacher of the deaf			○				
(b) Engraver						○	
12. (a) Organization and methods analyst							○
(b) Veterinary surgeon					○		
13. (a) Chemist					○		
(b) Statistician							○
14. (a) Youth club leader		○					
(b) Union negotiator				○			
15. (a) Dietician					○		
(b) Politician				○			
16. (a) Architect		○					
(b) Missionary				○			
17. (a) Estate agent				○			
(b) Community warden		○					
18. (a) Social worker			○				
(b) Editor	○						
19. (a) Interior decorator		○					
(b) Chemist					○		
20. (a) Press agent				○			
(b) Nuclear physicist					○		

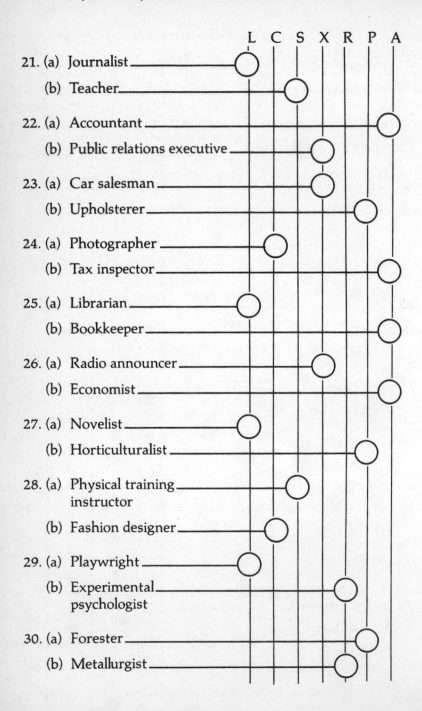

L C S X R P A

21. (a) Journalist
    (b) Teacher

22. (a) Accountant
    (b) Public relations executive

23. (a) Car salesman
    (b) Upholsterer

24. (a) Photographer
    (b) Tax inspector

25. (a) Librarian
    (b) Bookkeeper

26. (a) Radio announcer
    (b) Economist

27. (a) Novelist
    (b) Horticulturalist

28. (a) Physical training
        instructor
    (b) Fashion designer

29. (a) Playwright
    (b) Experimental
        psychologist

30. (a) Forester
    (b) Metallurgist

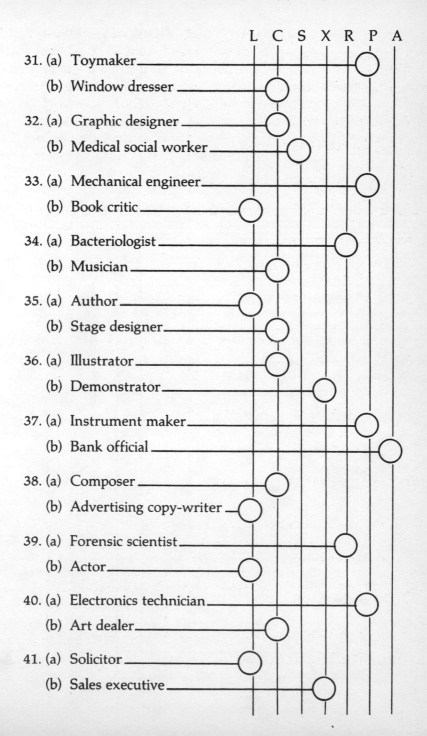

	L	C	S	X	R	P	A
31. (a) Toymaker						○	
(b) Window dresser		○					
32. (a) Graphic designer		○					
(b) Medical social worker			○				
33. (a) Mechanical engineer						○	
(b) Book critic	○						
34. (a) Bacteriologist					○		
(b) Musician		○					
35. (a) Author	○						
(b) Stage designer		○					
36. (a) Illustrator		○					
(b) Demonstrator				○			
37. (a) Instrument maker						○	
(b) Bank official							○
38. (a) Composer		○					
(b) Advertising copy-writer	○						
39. (a) Forensic scientist					○		
(b) Actor	○						
40. (a) Electronics technician						○	
(b) Art dealer		○					
41. (a) Solicitor	○						
(b) Sales executive				○			

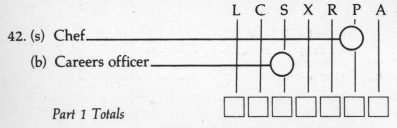

	L	C	S	X	R	P	A
42. (s) Chef						◯	
(b) Careers officer			◯				

Part 1 Totals

(not to be completed until Part 2 of the motivation questionnaire has been done)

Part 2

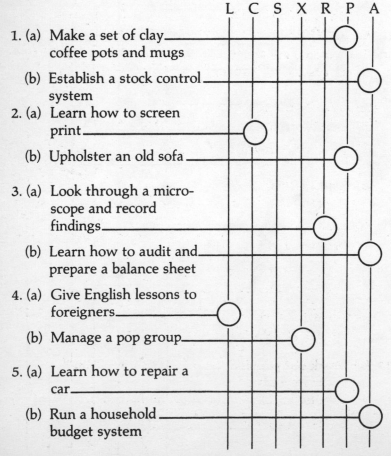

	L	C	S	X	R	P	A
1. (a) Make a set of clay coffee pots and mugs						◯	
(b) Establish a stock control system							◯
2. (a) Learn how to screen print		◯					
(b) Upholster an old sofa						◯	
3. (a) Look through a microscope and record findings					◯		
(b) Learn how to audit and prepare a balance sheet							◯
4. (a) Give English lessons to foreigners	◯						
(b) Manage a pop group				◯			
5. (a) Learn how to repair a car						◯	
(b) Run a household budget system							◯

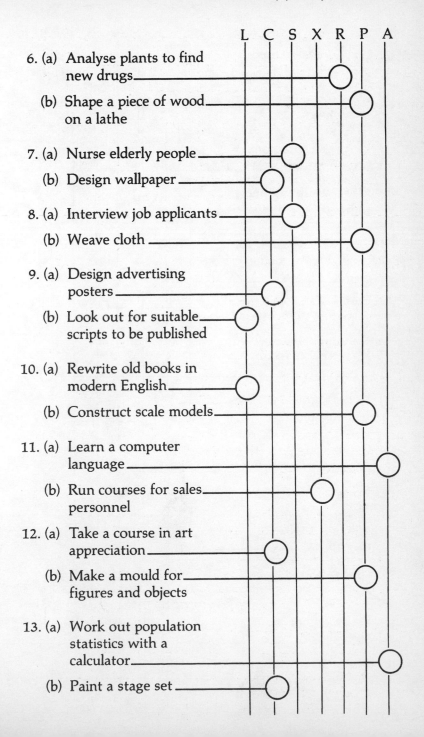

L C S X R P A

6. (a) Analyse plants to find new drugs

   (b) Shape a piece of wood on a lathe

7. (a) Nurse elderly people

   (b) Design wallpaper

8. (a) Interview job applicants

   (b) Weave cloth

9. (a) Design advertising posters

   (b) Look out for suitable scripts to be published

10. (a) Rewrite old books in modern English

    (b) Construct scale models

11. (a) Learn a computer language

    (b) Run courses for sales personnel

12. (a) Take a course in art appreciation

    (b) Make a mould for figures and objects

13. (a) Work out population statistics with a calculator

    (b) Paint a stage set

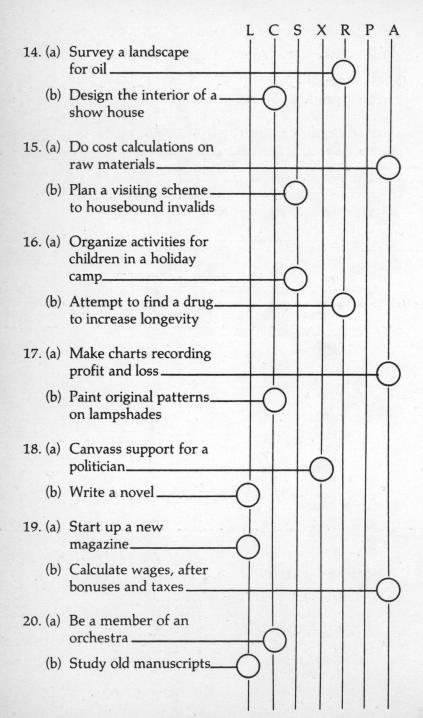

L C S X R P A

14. (a) Survey a landscape for oil

(b) Design the interior of a show house

15. (a) Do cost calculations on raw materials

(b) Plan a visiting scheme to housebound invalids

16. (a) Organize activities for children in a holiday camp

(b) Attempt to find a drug to increase longevity

17. (a) Make charts recording profit and loss

(b) Paint original patterns on lampshades

18. (a) Canvass support for a politician

(b) Write a novel

19. (a) Start up a new magazine

(b) Calculate wages, after bonuses and taxes

20. (a) Be a member of an orchestra

(b) Study old manuscripts

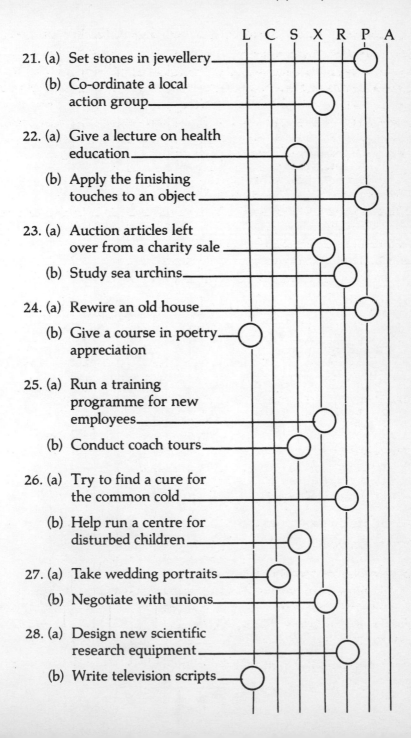

	L	C	S	X	R	P	A
21. (a) Set stones in jewellery						○	
(b) Co-ordinate a local action group				○			
22. (a) Give a lecture on health education			○				
(b) Apply the finishing touches to an object						○	
23. (a) Auction articles left over from a charity sale				○			
(b) Study sea urchins					○		
24. (a) Rewire an old house						○	
(b) Give a course in poetry appreciation	○						
25. (a) Run a training programme for new employees				○			
(b) Conduct coach tours			○				
26. (a) Try to find a cure for the common cold					○		
(b) Help run a centre for disturbed children			○				
27. (a) Take wedding portraits		○					
(b) Negotiate with unions				○			
28. (a) Design new scientific research equipment					○		
(b) Write television scripts	○						

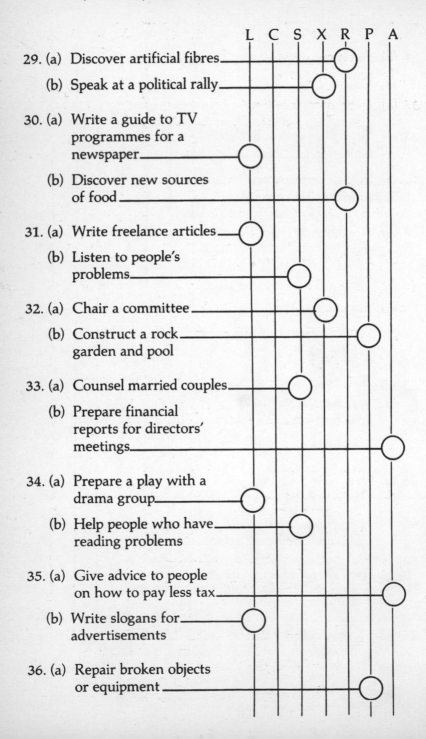

	L	C	S	X	R	P	A
29. (a) Discover artificial fibres					○		
(b) Speak at a political rally				○			
30. (a) Write a guide to TV programmes for a newspaper	○						
(b) Discover new sources of food					○		
31. (a) Write freelance articles	○						
(b) Listen to people's problems			○				
32. (a) Chair a committee				○			
(b) Construct a rock garden and pool						○	
33. (a) Counsel married couples			○				
(b) Prepare financial reports for directors' meetings							○
34. (a) Prepare a play with a drama group	○						
(b) Help people who have reading problems			○				
35. (a) Give advice to people on how to pay less tax							○
(b) Write slogans for advertisements	○						
36. (a) Repair broken objects or equipment						○	

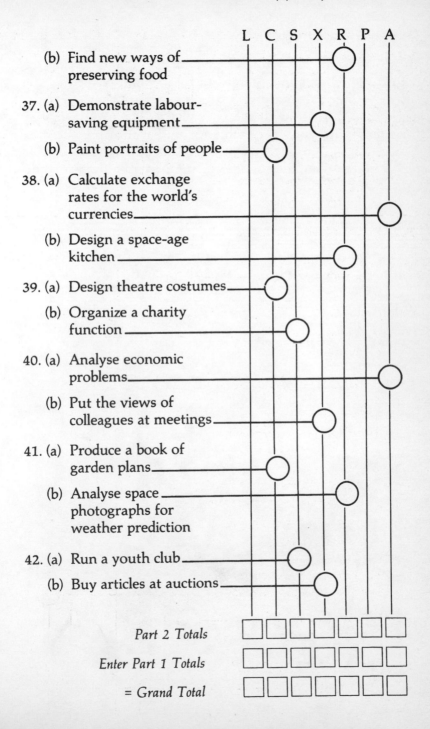

	L	C	S	X	R	P	A
(b) Find new ways of preserving food					○		
37. (a) Demonstrate labour-saving equipment				○			
(b) Paint portraits of people		○					
38. (a) Calculate exchange rates for the world's currencies							○
(b) Design a space-age kitchen					○		
39. (a) Design theatre costumes		○					
(b) Organize a charity function			○				
40. (a) Analyse economic problems							○
(b) Put the views of colleagues at meetings				○			
41. (a) Produce a book of garden plans		○					
(b) Analyse space photographs for weather prediction					○		
42. (a) Run a youth club			○				
(b) Buy articles at auctions				○			
Part 2 Totals	□	□	□	□	□	□	□
Enter Part 1 Totals	□	□	□	□	□	□	□
= Grand Total	□	□	□	□	□	□	□

The motivation graph

Turn first to the answers you gave in Part 1 and add up the figures in each column. Start with the column headed by the letter L. Count the total and put the figure at the bottom of the page. Do the same with the C, S, X, R, P and A columns. Continue in this way for each page until you can enter your total for Part 1 in the box provided. If you have done this correctly the combined scores of the seven columns should come to 126.

Do exactly the same with Part 2. Again, the column totals should equal 126. Now add the totals for the two parts together to get a grand total.

You can mark your score on the motivation graph on the next page. You will now see what the capital letters stand for. Draw a line across the point where your score falls. Do this with all seven scores. Then shade upwards from the bottom of the graph to this point. You will then have a profile of your motivation. It may look something like the graph below.

Your motivation graph

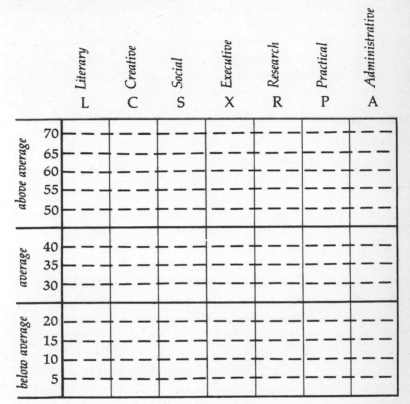

Interpreting your motivational results

Do your graphical results make sense to you? They should provide you with a system of preferences, a hierarchy which ranges from the strongest area of attraction to the weakest. The simplest way to proceed from here is to suggest that you pursue your areas of high motivation and avoid your low ones.

Look at both your high and your low scores. What is high or low will depend upon your own profile, but most people get some scores which are in the 'above average' range as well as some which are in the 'below average' range. If some of your scores are 'average', this indicates that you do not currently have particularly strong feelings one way or the other about this sphere of activity.

For most people a score higher than 48 suggests strong motivation and of course the higher the score, the stronger the preference for that occupational area. Conversely, scores below 24 will usually indicate areas which have very little appeal to you. Unless you feel you'd like to know more about what is actually involved in terms of work, you should probably avoid them.

You may have been asking yourself why there were two parts to the motivation questionnaire. The aim was to get as broad a picture as possible of you. The first part was based on the career titles which might appeal to you and the second dealt with career activities associated with them. The closer the scores you gained in Parts 1 and 2, the clearer your conception of your motivation will be. If there is a wide discrepancy between the two scores in any area of motivation, this would suggest that your knowledge of careers in the area concerned is not very high. A difference of more than about ten points does not matter but a wider discrepancy may indicate that your motivation will change once you know more about the careers which fall into this category.

If there are no great differences in your scores – that is, no sharply defined extremes – this means either (a) you do not know very much about yourself, (b) you do not know what is involved in different areas of work, (c) you may be multi-talented but helpless in the face of so many opportunities, or (d) nothing much appeals to you at all! In all these instances, the ability and personality tests will be of greater value in defining what would motivate you if you were more aware of your potential.

What happens if your motivation results appear to be saying that you do not like the career you are in, eg if you are a business executive and your results seem to indicate that you want to be an artist? Do you give everything up and move to the Left Bank in Paris? Not at all. The questionnaire is subtle and the answers it gives are sometimes directional rather than specific. In this case, it is not necessarily saying that your present job is wrong for you, merely that you would like more opportunity to do things your own way, to be creative. Perhaps you can achieve this in your present work, with a little reorientation. Or perhaps you really should give it all up and move to the *Rive Gauche*. In the end, you are the best person to evaluate the real meaning of your results: you are the one who has to make the decisions.

Some people obtain one strong area of motivation which makes interpretation comparatively simple. Others get two or even three peaks of motivation so that having to combine these in a career becomes much more difficult. In fact, if there are three areas it may be useful to consult a careers counsellor to help you make sense of your results (though you should be able to put the elements together more or less by yourself). Take time to think through your results and ask yourself, 'What could I do which is basically concerned with ..., but which has a little of ... and where I am occasionally involved with ...?' You may find yourself becoming quite inventive. And truth to say, there are many jobs which contain numerous elements, so it is by no means impossible to find a job which contains all the pieces you require to motivate you fully.

The following pages contain broad areas of career motivation, together with lists of careers which fit roughly into them. Within each area there are careers of great diversity. For example, in the Practical area you will find both lock keeper and locksmith. The former is involved in outdoor work which often requires heavy physical movement; the latter works mainly indoors and the mechanical movements are frequently intricate. Look at the seven major areas of motivation and you can then break each career down further to see which part of it would or would not appeal. In doing so, you might find that the Practical area appeals to you most, but you might reject an individual career because it is perhaps too administrative or not sufficiently concerned with people, and so on. The process is taken a step further when later on in this chapter the seven broad areas of motivation are broken down yet again into combined areas of motivation.

First we focus on your highest peak of motivation. It is important that you attend to this most of all, because this is where you are likely to achieve your greatest satisfaction. Next we look at the major combinations of motivational areas and see what careers may be appropriate. You could well find yourself looking up three or even four areas having located your motivation in the matrix below.

Primary areas of motivation

	L	C	S	X	R	P	A
L	1						
C		2					
S			3				
X				4			
R					5		
P						6	
A							7

1. Literary

You are attracted by careers involving words, ideas and communication. You will be happy reading or writing a lot – probably both. Other interests or activities might also appeal, but these can be saved for leisure time. It is with a literary activity that you want to spend most of your time.

You probably have some background or experience in this area already. Your favourite subject at school may well have been English or something closely related to it, such as history. The lessons you enjoyed most were those in which you constructed essays or had a chance to write creatively. You have probably written a few short stories at some time in your life or tried your hand at poetry. Words fascinate you and you enjoy knowing their meanings as well as using them precisely.

If you have not been engaged in literary events hitherto, it is possible that your self-awareness has changed. Perhaps now is the time to find out whether you have any talent. Some people have produced a first novel after retirement.

As well as the specifically 'literary' careers there are other associated careers which are easier to get into. Very few of us can expect to be great poets but we may reasonably expect to be wordsmiths of some kind.

Some careers in this area do depend on exceptional talent – for example, those of author, poet and dramatist. But success in these areas rarely just happens; it often requires years of practice as well as the ability to cope with failure. Other careers depend much more upon academic qualifications. At the professional level, a certain amount of specialized study is likely to be a requirement (as in the case of librarian or journalist). If you can combine your literary motivation with another there are careers at all levels, particularly in the administrative area. There are more opportunities to work with words in everyday administration and communication than in the area of literary aesthetics.

Careers

actor/actress	language teacher
editor	librarian
historian	literary critic
interpreter	novelist
journalist	proof reader

2. Creative

You want a career in which you can express yourself creatively but not with words so much as in music or some form of fine art. Your medium is visual or oral as opposed to verbal. Beauty and aesthetics are your passions.

Many people are attracted by careers in this area because they sound exciting. The opportunity to express ourselves has a universal appeal, though comparatively few can make a living from art – at least in its purest forms. But we like the sound of the creative lifestyle, with its overtones of Bohemianism and iconoclasm. The discipline actually to be a successful artist is another thing altogether, especially when the audience we would like to applaud us remains unappreciative!

Do you have the talent? What evidence is there? The ability tests are less helpful in this area because success will depend upon popular taste and fashion rather than specific mental aptitudes; it is hard to set an examination in creative potential. In popular music, a feel for what many people will enjoy listening to is the key, whereas a formal scholarship from a music school carries no guarantee of success.

Maybe you feel that your budding talent was never developed at school and was stifled later when you had to put the need to earn a living first. It is probably easier to start late with art than music, though there are few rules in this area; determination and a belief in yourself are the essential prerequisites.

There are few opportunities for those who want to live solely by presenting their own work. You will need to be prepared to sacrifice income as well as security on a full-time basis. There is more stability in a design team, or in an orchestra, as a member of the theatre or TV production team. You may be able to compromise without sacrificing your ideals. Do you need to make your own 'statement' or can you be content giving people what they enjoy? For example, you could apply your art in such areas as the practical – thus making it into a craft, or in the social – by becoming a teacher. If self-expression is essential and you would be discontent using your art to provide a service rather than presenting it for its own sake, the following are some of the few opportunities open to you:

Careers

architect	interior designer
artist	make-up artist

dancer	musician
dressmaker	sculptor
engraver	silversmith
florist	vision mixer
goldsmith	window dresser
illustrator	

3. Social

Your main interest lies in helping or assisting others. You are keen to see them develop, improve themselves and become self-reliant. You are prepared to subordinate your own wishes to the service of others. It is not simply a question of being with people – there are lots of careers in which you might be more popular – but of viewing the needs of others as the end product of your work.

How well and in what ways do you develop relationships with others? Have you an obviously caring nature, seeing your own reward in the natural enjoyment and benefit others derive from your attention? Or perhaps you are a more detached type with some need to do something for others without getting too personally involved. Nearly all the social careers have some kind of emotional involvement. If your feelings are easily bruised it may be better to give this area a miss. A strong personality is often required just in order to cope and it may take a thicker skin than you realize.

It is sensible to get some experience before taking up a career in this area. In the ordinary way there is very little available to help you to make up your mind. Your schooldays were largely intended to develop you scholastically – vocational training related to social service is unlikely to have had a place, important though it may be. Have you enjoyed babysitting? Have you been an assistant at a summer camp, a scoutmaster or guide leader, a voluntary helper or a prison visitor? If so, you are on the right lines.

There are lots of careers in the social area as so many of the nation's resources are devoted to education, training, health and welfare programmes. Some jobs require extensive training as well as natural interpersonal skills: you need professional qualifications for social work, teaching and almost all the jobs in which responsibility for others is directly dependent upon your judgement. We expect our general practitioners to be highly competent. The more the job becomes advisory or of an assisting nature as opposed to influential and controlling, the less essential the qualifications.

Careers

ambulance crew	nurse
careers adviser	nursery nurse
chiropodist	osteopath
doctor	physiotherapist
educational psychologist	probation officer
health visitor	remedial teacher
hostel warden	social worker
industrial nurse	teacher (infant/junior)
midwife	

4. Executive

You are motivated by activities in which you can organize and influence others. You will want to have responsibility for managing others as well as making decisions about what should be done and how it should be done.

Some executive responsibility can be found in many careers, but if this kind of motivation is a distinctive feature you are clearly ambitious. For example, you are likely to be pushy and even aggressive at times in order to get what you want. If your motivation peak is very high you are unlikely to be content as 'second in command'. You will want to see some tangible evidence of your success in getting to the top and therefore material rewards are very important to you.

Even though our educational system is both extensive and highly structured, people who pursue careers in the executive area are not necessarily academic or even highly qualified;

success depends a good deal upon hard-to-define qualities such as flair and initiative.

Do you have experience of spotting opportunities, particularly for making some extra money, and then making something of them? People with this motivation don't wait for things to happen – they make them happen. You might have any kind of background and any kind of talent: you could be an executive in a creative area such as film making, or an administrative area such as banking, or in numerous others. The essential characteristic of this motivation is the will to succeed, wherever you find yourself. Thus, if your background is in research, you may see an opportunity to exploit your research commercially; if you are in welfare administration, you may feel you might do better for yourself in the private sector.

Careers

business consultant	personnel director
export salesperson	political agent
management consultant	politician
managing director	retail manager
marketing manager	sales manager
negotiator	team manager

5. Research

This attraction shows how much you enjoy acquiring knowledge. As a result of this you seem prepared to devote a great deal of time to study and the careers which appeal to you generally need academic, professional or special qualifications. It is likely that you are curious about why things happen as they do. You do not like making guesses – you like to find reasons. You enjoy applying facts and arriving at solutions through logic and analytical investigation.

At school, you would have preferred scientific subjects, particularly the mainstream disciplines of mathematics, physics, chemistry and biology. You will have enjoyed objective problem solving and being able to sift through information in order to draw conclusions. You will have enjoyed experimenting and working with formulae.

Many people admire the intellectual rigour required in careers connected with research, and it is not everyone who possesses the patience and discipline to do well. These careers are difficult to take up as second careers since most training follows directly from subjects studied at school. Again, the demands of the training are such that it is preferable to undertake it before other responsibilities, such as a family, make study more difficult. There is also some justification to the theory that the best researchers do their most important work – make their breakthrough – in their early twenties.

The pursuit of a career in this area inevitably makes you into something of a specialist. There are few opportunities for general scientists, although some people have made a living by writing popular books which explain various scientific theories to lay people in an interesting way. Generally, you will need to be able to sustain an interest in a narrow part of science, possibly within the same institution or with the same employer for most of your career. The country is crying out for more scientists and technologists, though the areas of demand do change; for example, computer science is currently more in demand than geology. As in any field, the top jobs are always highly competitive.

Careers

astronomer
bacteriologist
botanist
chemist
dietitian
ergonomist
experimental psychologist
forensic scientist
laboratory technician

material scientist
mathematician
meteorologist
microbiologist
ophthalmist
physicist
radiographer
surgeon

6. Practical

Motivation in this area shows that you want to be up and doing. By contrast, a sedentary career is likely to have little appeal: it would confine you or give you too little opportunity to actually make something. In fact there are two strong elements to a practical motivation, and it is possible to have one without the other and still get a high score on the questionnaire.

The first is that you may want to be out and about as well as physically involved, so that labour of some kind might be involved. The second element is the need to work with your hands, whether in a rugged or a precise and highly skilled way. In either case, you probably enjoy touching materials and constructing objects. You may have a technical or craft interest and at times this can approach the artistic. Although you may be less obviously a craftsman you will still enjoy being active and mobile and you will no doubt take pride in the employment of physical skills.

How good are you with your hands? Do you enjoy intricate operations or working on a large scale? Some natural talent or affinity with materials or the environment is often detectable at an early age. Do you like shaping, cutting, or moulding with wood or clay? Or do you prefer engines and equipment?

Whether you work with natural or artificial materials, whether your interest is in a craft or simply in being active, there are opportunities at all levels. Some careers have years of study as a prerequisite whereas others depend upon experience and polished manual dexterity. A sure eye and a careful pair of hands might be enough for some, while others require a theoretical understanding as well.

A distinctive feature of careers in this area is the isolation which often characterizes them: the forester, the driver and the diver work largely alone. Other careers may still require individual skills but also involve co-ordinating individual efforts with those of others in a productive team effort. A number of the craft skills relating to the building trade fall into this category.

Careers

animal keeper	guard
blacksmith/farrier	gunsmith
boat builder	instrument maker
builder	jockey
butcher	joiner
carpenter	lighthouse keeper
coastguard	lock keeper
cook	locksmith
diver	mechanic
driver	merchant sailor
farmer	miner
firefighter	nature conservancy warden
fisherman	oil rig worker
fitter	shipping pilot
forester	traffic warden
gamekeeper	upholsterer
groom	veterinary nurse
groundskeeper	

7. Administrative

This is a broad area of motivation covering business finance and office administration. It has to do with the running of an organization whether a private enterprise or a public institution, and involves the organization of people, resources and information.

To be successful you need to be orderly and systematic, though not in the same way as the scientist; your goal is to be an organizer, co-ordinator and adviser in a commercial setting, however loosely that may be defined. Administrators 'know what is going on' within the organization and they make information available to those who need it. They rarely make strategic policy decisions themselves. You will know the value of qualifications and hence your own market worth. It is rare for people to succeed in large organizations unless they have the recognized qualifications of the relevant professional institute: insurance requires insurance exams, banking requires banking exams, accounting requires accounting exams and so on. It is possible to work your way up within an organization but increasingly it seems preferable to extend one's education before embarking upon a professional career. For example, professional accountants have recently found themselves at a disadvantage when competing for jobs against accountants who also possess a degree.

Administration as an activity is changing since it now frequently requires people-related skills (the 'over-the-counter' manner) or different technical skills (eg computer literacy). Nevertheless, the key motivation is the same as for a career connected with some aspect of financial, legal, commercial or business organization. High-level administrative jobs involve running large organizations and there are many types of work available in banking, insurance and economics as well as in all areas of business.

Careers

accountant	cashier
accounting technician	clerk
actuary	company secretary
administrator	industrial relations officer
auditor	legal executive
bank clerk	purser
bookkeeper	records clerk
building society manager/	securities analyst
assistant	tax inspector
bursar	

Combined patterns of motivation

A distinct peak of motivation will show you where your major direction lies but a second or even third peak may reveal a key emphasis you would like to see in your work. In fact, although your own motivation may be very clear, it is rare to find a career that does not contain several elements. This is where matching yourself to a career becomes more complicated, but it need not be difficult if you take the structured approach we use in this book. It is as well to read not only the major patterns of motivation but also the combinations given below. In this way, you can think about extremes of possibilities and then narrow these down until you get the correct focus.

Combined areas of motivation

	L	C	S	X	R	P	A
L	1						
C	8	2					
S	14	9	3				
X	19	15	10	4			
R	23	20	16	11	5		
P	26	24	21	17	12	6	
A	28	27	25	22	18	13	7

8. Creative and literary

This combination shows motivation careers with an intellectual content. Your interest will primarily be for ideas rather than for material things. You will want to have an outlet for personal expression and to work in an imaginative or creative environment. This does not necessarily mean a rejection of reality, only that the emphasis of your work should be aesthetic.

In fact, careers in this area may range from the almost totally aesthetic to the high-gloss 'media' jobs. Your personal direction will be influenced by how much of your remaining motivation tends towards the executive or the administrative.

Careers

actor/actress	film reviewer
advertising copywriter	TV production assistant
dramatist	

9. Social and creative

This combination of preferences brings together sensitivity towards art and a caring relationship with others. Work in this area demands patience, tact and emotional warmth. In careers requiring this combination art will generally take second place to the social requirement; it is used as a means or technique for helping, not as an end in itself.

There are few opportunities available and those which do exist are not very highly paid. In fact, much of the work in this area is done on a part-time or voluntary basis. A good deal of selflessness is required; you will also need organizing ability, though executive and administrative motivation are not likely to feature highly. Some practical motivation may often appear as well. These jobs are for people who want to use their skill in a caring environment for the welfare of others. They may be involved in improving a person's physical co-ordination or mental health as well as with artistic appreciation and educational development.

Careers

art therapist	nursery teacher
music therapist	occupational therapist

10. Social and executive

If you have this combination of preferences then you obviously have a need to work with people. This is less likely to be in a caring or obviously helping relationship than in business or administrative management. You will probably prefer the business to the public sector, though this is not always so. Your preferences for working with, and almost definitely through, people will be even clearer if at the same time you reject areas of work in which you would be in contact with things, objects, numbers or ideas.

Those with this combination should be socially skilled and usually they are: make sure these preferences do not arise simply because you would like to have talents that in fact you do not possess! Careers in this area are generally for people with a background of social service who want more influence and who enjoy managing or organizing.

Careers

director of social services	job interviewer
funeral director	retail manager
head teacher of large school	salesperson
hotel manager	

11. Executive and research

This is an unusual combination of preferences which are often thought to be mutually exclusive. People who hold one set do not usually hold the other. It is the association of the intellectual in direct juxtaposition with the commercial that is apparently so odd. If you have pursued a career with a research bias you have followed a course of study and will have denied yourself personal gain of a material or political kind. Most research careers are directed towards coming up with information of some kind. They therefore constitute a back-up expert service which is commercially exploited by those whose motivation is inherently of a different kind. The commercialization of science is an expensive business; there are few opportunities to simply 'start up' on your own. Recently there has been a growth in computer-related businesses, which are often started up at relatively little cost. However, it is much more difficult to start up a new business in one of the traditional sciences. One of the problems businesses have is to identify the entrepreneurs with a technical/scientific background – so if you have these preferences, you could well be a valuable property!

Careers

director of private research
dispensing optician
general chemist

manager of computer bureau
technical representative
veterinary surgeon

12. Research and practical

If this is your combination, you will enjoy the application of science. Research will be empty theory, merely cold abstraction, unless it can be brought to bear on some physical problem and achieve something. You may well work with people and a business but your interest is with the equipment and technology. You will be scientific, but will also enjoy working skilfully with your hands. You like to see things happen, to produce concrete end results. There could also be a preference for activity – you like to get out and about and see science at work in the environment. There are few careers for which study and professional status are not prerequisites.

Careers

agriculturalist
bio medical engineer
computer engineer
engineer
environmental health officer
ergonomist
geologist
horologist

hydrologist
metallurgist
navigating officer
scientific instrument maker
surveyor
technologist
work study officer

13. Practical and administrative

Is it possible to be at the same time active and involved in office work? Careers which are normally considered sedentary appear to be incompatible with those connected with handling materials and equipment. Usually it can only be managed, if at all, by some kind of 'trade off' arrangement, such as spending 50 per cent or thereabouts of your time in each environment. Thus you may go out to do your work and then return to your office to compile a report. It is often the case that people in these careers view the administrative side as the 'necessary evil' because their hearts are more passionately located in the practical and active elements of their work.

Careers

agricultural secretary	office machinery mechanic
baths manager	organization and methods
builder's merchant	officer
customs officer	rating valuation officer
manufacturing	storekeeper
superintendent	

14. Literary and social

This pattern shows a desire for a career combining the opportunity to help others with some involvement in ideas. It may be a case of transmitting ideas to others with the aim of enlightening them or of encouraging them to communicate and express themselves in their own right. Most jobs have a connection with teaching and usually demand some expert skill with languages, either of an oral or written kind – often both. The emphasis, whether literary or social, varies in different jobs: the art form or literary subject may be the principal attraction and this will define the social form, which could be a class meeting together for literary appreciation or to learn a language. Alternatively, language or a related subject may be used as an aid to the mental development and emotional capability of others, as in so many forms of teaching and therapy.

Careers

interviewer	speech therapist
language teacher	training officer
liberal studies teacher	

15. Creative and executive

So you want to be involved with art and make money too? It seems that life is going to be varied and exciting whatever your values and ideals. You will want a stimulating and expressive environment but you also require some recognizable signs of material success. You will enjoy the elaborate expression of ideas even though they may be temporary. You will be concerned with style and with novelty. You will be competitive and enjoy taking risks, preferring careers where the demands are continually changing or where there is always a sensational element. You will therefore reject routine activities and you want to make your own decisions on key issues. People with this kind of motivation are often opinionated and prefer to leave details, as well as facts and figures, to others. They regard themselves as self-starters and often leave the 'finishing off' to other people. It is possible that you will be inspired and will often be able to persuade others; you will enjoy having influence and converting others to your tastes.

Careers

advertising account executive	brand manager
art dealer	fashion buyer
	media director

16. Social and research

The application of scientific knowledge and techniques in the service of others is what appeals to you. Although you have plenty of contact with other people your expertise will keep you detached and your role will often be advisory. Your assistance to others is therefore much more likely to be of a material or informational kind rather than of a qualitative type involving any great degree of direct emotional input. You will require personal skills, such as tact and understanding, though you are unlikely to maintain a continually caring involvement. You will have a record of success with analytical and statistical subjects but are probably too outgoing to be content with pure research work. However, the emphasis, as the examples below show, varies widely.

Careers

clinical psychologist	orthoptist
dental assistant	radiographer
dentist	science teacher
nurse	social science researcher

17. Executive and practical

You want to be involved with administration and commerce but without being confined to an office. Though office work of some kind is likely to be necessary, you will not often be found behind the desk. Rather, you will be out of doors viewing, estimating or managing on site. There are a number of entrepreneurial activities relating to the land and agricultural products as well as careers in property and equipment. You may be involved in running a large enterprise such as an estate or alternatively you could be a one-man band. It is usual to combine education with practical experience and there is no point in thinking of careers in these areas unless you can turn your hand to most things, fixing them yourself or getting them going. You will need to be enterprising as well as able to recognize the value of commodities and materials.

Careers

accident assessor	production manager
auctioneer	publican
demonstrator	transport manager
estate agent	undertaker
farm manager	

18. Research and administrative

This combination would involve you with facts and figures. You will want to deal with information and your approach to problem-solving will be systematic and logical. The pattern is particularly clear when little value is set upon the people-related or more intuitive areas of motivation. Thus you will want to deal with data, applying analytical methods in administrative and commercial settings.

You are very well placed if you have these preferences. There has recently been an expansion of office systems which is fortunate for you! Indeed, in some areas the technocrat appears to be superseding conventional roles. For example, in banking, computer experts are now obtaining senior posts where once only years of banking experience would have sufficed. You may be sought after as an expert providing back-up services. If you have entrepreneurial motivation as well, then perhaps some 'leading edge' information technology business would suit you – there is such a demand that many have started up. If you also have a welfare interest look for opportunities in areas of training.

Careers

business systems analyst   operational researcher
computer programmer   statistician
economist   systems analyst
market researcher

19. Literary and executive

This combines an interest in ideas and communication with the chance of exploiting these in business. There may be a specific involvement in books or at least with the spoken or written word. You may be keen on writing yourself and will certainly be very appreciative of it. It is difficult to have a career in this area without a background in media, which often follows an academic background. Your studies are likely to have been in literature, languages, history, law or related areas. The careers which attract you are highly competitive and frequently demanding of the highest intellectual as well as entrepreneurial skills. Few opportunities exist at anything but the highest levels.

Sometimes these preferences are combined with administration, which shows a leaning more towards the business organization side. If on the other hand your bias is towards the creative it will show that the thrust of your interest is more intellectually driven.

Careers

conference executive   public relations manager
literary agent   publisher
newspaper editor/manager   radio or TV producer

20. Creative and research

You are unlikely to be able to pursue your motivation with this combination unless you have both skill and training, which can be either from the artistic or scientific side. You want to combine the two in your career and this makes you unusual, because these areas are often thought to be mutually exclusive. However, art can be close to engineering – for example in car styling, as in so many other manufacturing operations. Many fine artists employed in the restoration of pictures need to know about chemical processes as well as about physics.

Careers

beautician   medical illustrator
cartographer   museum assistant
designer   photographer
draughtsperson   restorer
lighting technician

21. Social and practical

Your interest is in people and you will want to do something for them which is practical and shows definite results. The environment you are in as well as the skills you possess enable you to be active. The pattern is more clearly defined if you reject the administrative areas of work as being too desk-bound for you. You may well be a good organizer but you like to carry things out and see them done so that in contrast with your practical management, your desk might be untidy and the paperwork forgotten. Your background might be in sports or you may have an artistic inclination. The 'people' content of the work varies a good deal, verging on the instructional at one end to the therapeutic at the other. But in the end it is an interest in people rather than the activity itself which will make you successful in these areas of work.

Careers

hairdresser	prison officer
masseur/masseuse	sports centre assistant
occupational therapist	team coach
police officer	youth leader

22. Executive and administrative

Success in this area often depends upon having a skills background in, for example, banking, insurance, commerce or office administration. The skills are taken further than would be required in a purely technical job because they will be used in management and business decision making. If you combine these preferences, you have a powerful drive to succeed in the business world. Possibly, artistic or welfare-related areas are less important to you as you will want to concern yourself with the 'real world'. Success depends largely upon your own efforts but the skills you have will help you get there – which in your case will be to the top! Your technical knowledge and professional background will make you a formidable force in the boardroom as you enter general management from a functional specialism. However, you will have a tendency to make decisions on the basis of evidence from the figures, and the 'commercial' side of business will interest you more than the outward-facing or media-related areas.

Careers

bank manager	insurance agent
broker	office manager
club manager	sales administrator
estate manager	tax consultant
film producer	turf accountant
finance director	underwriter

23. Literary and research

You may be able to combine these preferences in a career which fuses science with art. In this case, you are likely to be highly qualified: you will be one of the lucky few who are very highly specialized and for whom there are careers available. Most careers will be in an academic or educational environment. If your background is in research you may also have a literary talent which allows you to write about your subject. Additional personal skills would be required if you are to be successful in presenting your work to others as a lecturer or a trainer.

Careers

anthropologist	science writer
archaeologist	technical writer
information scientist	

24. Creative and practical

These preferences come together more harmoniously than most. You will enjoy the practical arts where design and beauty can be employed in a useful way. This may be as additional decoration to materials or as an intrinsic part of the material or product itself. Your interests verge closely upon craft activities but are distinguished from them because they are utilitarian although, admittedly, crafts often have a beauty of their own.

The activities which interest you are often practised in isolation or within a group of like-minded people. They are not social or material so you will probably reject those areas which connect you with commerce. You may occasionally be able to see a way of combining your motivation with teaching or in some form of business. There is rarely a career structure and much depends upon whether you have both the skill and a definite idea of the lifestyle which would satisfy you.

Careers

book-binder	engineering pattern maker
cabinet maker	film projectionist
cameraman	flyman
confectioner	gardener
dresser	jewellery maker
embalmer	pattern cutter
embroiderer	picture framer

25. Social and administrative

Work in which the object is to help others appeals to you but you will want to bring together resources to make this happen. Although you may have a caring temperament yourself, your preference is to arrange services rather than get involved in a direct way. You are often a supplies officer helping those in the front line, such as teachers or social workers for example. You will want to administer a system which provides people with resources. In this area of work it is often difficult to satisfy others, and indeed you may have to reconcile yourself to the fact that you cannot always help personally: you will only get involved as far as is legally or contractually permitted. However, cases where personal judgement is required occur frequently and you will gain satisfaction from knowing and applying the system to the benefit of others.

Careers

courier/local representative	medical secretary
employment officer	principal nursing officer

26. Literary and practical

These two preferences do not combine easily in one career: when you think about it, it is difficult to see how writing and being active can take place at the same time! You have to leave one before you can do the other. It may in fact be the case that you will reconcile this by having two quite separate careers. Alternatively, one may simply have to be left to your leisure time – and which one will in the end be determined by the stronger preference.

   If you want a career with this combination, you will probably have to follow one or the other preference and then transpose it into the alternative setting. To give some examples, an agricultural secretary does the same work as other secretaries but is out and about more in the country; a printer has a mechanical and increasingly technical job where the end product is words (although he or she does not need to be 'literary' as such).

Careers

agricultural secretary   technical writer
printer

27. Creative and administrative

You may be creative in your own right but need to be a good organizer and aware of costs to do your job effectively; you may have a background in office work but want to be part of a creative enterprise. Your job might be of the type which provides back-up or support to others, but in some cases you might have to take a leading role. Thus, a chef has a good deal of decision making, as does a merchandiser.

Careers

chef   studio assistant
choreographer's assistant   theatre administrator
cinema manager   theatre box office clerk
merchandiser   wardrobe manager

28. Literary and administrative

This combination directs you towards many possible careers. It relates to those which are largely to do with communications where the emphasis is upon figures, and is often a haven for people whose initial interest and background or training was literary, but who came to the conclusion that business was likely to be a more rewarding environment for them. Alternatively, for those with an administrative background the literary element gives wider opportunities. Careers range from executive to professional positions at all levels. There are opportunities in areas of public service, the private sector and the media. It is a very broad combination and you may need to study the rest of your motivational pattern to decide exactly where your emphases should be.

Careers

administrator (clerical/ executive)	legal executive
	library assistant
barrister	secretary
company secretary	solicitor
entertainments officer	receptionist

Who I will become – Applying my potential

Ability, personality and motivation all need to be considered in combination. It would be unwise to simply head off in the direction of what you most want to do without taking into account what you are most capable of doing, whether the job will continue to appeal and to what extent your personality will determine your success. There is little point in taking up a career which provides an intellectual challenge in the short term if your personality is of a type which enjoys making use of interpersonal skills or if you have an entrepreneurial drive towards success.

This book has given you three structured ways of analysing yourself and making deductions about your career: it is now time to put these structures together to form a realistic action plan. There may be some inconsistencies in the three structures which need to be resolved and your own life situation may mean that some compromises have to be made. For example, what do you do if your intellectual talent is greatest for numbers and you have low motivation for careers in administration or research? What if you like the idea of being a diver but appear to have no mechanical ability? And what if the idea of an outdoor occupation appeals to you but your experience since leaving school 20 years ago has been in banking?

Whatever your particular circumstances and whatever the unique make-up of your intelligence, personality and motivation, the structured approach you have pursued through this book should guide you in the most logical way towards a suitable career.

We have found one simple overriding principle: use all your aptitudes to their maximum. Undersell yourself at your peril! So if your aptitudes are high, don't deny them because you will eventually be bored. In general, the more you get on and do what you want to do and know what you can do, the happier and more respectful of yourself you will be.

Case study 1: The ex-teacher

Amanda was 37. She had once been a teacher but left work in order to have a family. Now she was divorced and faced increasingly with the responsibility of providing for herself and her two children, one of whom was in senior school and the other well into junior school. Although she had worked for several successful years as a teacher before having a family, the idea of returning to teaching was unattractive. She had thought of herself as a good teacher but felt that the present-day demands on teachers would involve her much more in caring or social work, which she did not think she would be good at. The following was her summary of herself after she had tested her aptitudes:

	least suitable	*most suitable*
Ability	technical	analytical numerical
Personality	aggressive pushy	calm feeling
Motivation	persuasive	administrative people scientific

Amanda was not surprised to find she had done well in the numerical and analytical tests because she had pursued sciences at school and had in fact been a biology teacher. It was her motivational results, showing a high preference for the administrative, which made her think of putting science to one side and moving into the administrative or office-based areas of work. She would still have the contact with people she enjoyed, though it looked as though she ought to avoid a business in which she would have to be persuasive personally or sell herself. The quality of contact she should have with others was made clearer by the personality test results, which showed her to be rather more on the feeling than the aggressive side. This was in tune with the way she thought of herself – as wanting to fit in with people rather than actually take charge of them. She felt she had a calm and matter-of-fact personality and it was this side of her that was probably attracted by administrative careers. Although there was some scientific motivation, she thought that what she liked about science was logic and being able to work in a systematic way – something which is clearly available in administration in the area of computers and office systems.

Amanda obtained a clerical job working in accounts and within a year had embarked upon accounting and administration courses at a local college in order to obtain qualifications in what she expects to be a satisfactory third career.

Case study 2: The test engineer

Alan had qualifications in mechanics and electronics. He was the team leader, undertaking qualitative analysis and research studies of the company's products, in a large international organization. Although his work had been interesting in the past and he had been told that it was highly valued by the company, he now felt that he was getting nowhere. Indeed, he still enjoyed the technology itself but he would have liked more say in what products were actually developed.

In addition, he felt that he would like more contact with the customers since he enjoyed the occasional but incidental contact he had with them as the technical expert. He had thought of leaving his present company and seeing if another might suit him better, but his wife was concerned about the impact that any relocation might have on their children's education and whether they could actually afford to move having recently taken on a large mortgage. These were his results on testing his aptitudes:

	least suitable	*most suitable*
Ability	acuity	technical analytical
Personality		factual group
Motivation	people creative	persuasive scientific administrative

Alan was interested to see that his personality was group-orientated. He enjoyed working with a team of people and in fact had on occasions been able to advise people who had come to him to discuss their personal difficulties. He had also liked joining social groups, but had had more opportunity for this outside than inside work. In fact, he began to wonder whether it might have been the lack of management opportunity at work that was beginning to frustrate him.

A further area of frustration was clarified when he saw that his motivational results included both a persuasive and an administrative interest as well as the scientific one that he had expected. This also indicated that he wanted more managerial responsibility in making decisions and influencing matters. The administrative interest made him think of a commercial as opposed to a purely technical role. It was clear that he wanted to change his career within the organization although the lack of any strong creative motivation seemed to indicate that a radical move into a different function, such as marketing or public relations, was unnecessary.

In fact, he persuaded his company to give him some experience in the area of service engineering. This allowed him to apply his knowledge in a practical way and gain some experience of the commercial world, as well as meeting customers. The job demanded skills he had never used before but which had always been dormant and he found he was able to extend his career in new and challenging ways. After a short time in which his career appeared to stand still because he had made a lateral rather than a vertical move, his career accelerated and he obtained a management role.

Case study 3: The college leaver

Joe had enjoyed obtaining a degree in Pure Mathematics. He had felt intellectually stimulated at university which he liked for all its aspects, including the social side. He had not only been a keen member of a sports team but had also participated in a debating society and was a leading light on the students' committee. He was uncertain what to do, although he had been offered a research post at the university which would not only pay him but lead on to a higher degree. However, he had a feeling that he had been too long a student and felt a hankering for the real world. Amid pressure from his parents, who were justly proud of him, and the expectations of his tutors, he saw no credible alternative until he tested his aptitudes:

	least suitable	*most suitable*
Ability	acuity technical	analytical numerical verbal
Personality	feeling	factual aggressive group
Motivation	scientific people	persuasive administrative creative

Joe's aptitudes were good but he saw little chance to use his verbal ability if he stayed in the academic world, except as a teacher or perhaps a writer. He felt he wanted to break away from the university environment and that his strong verbal ability held the promise of a job where communication and dealing with people would play a large rather than just an occasional part. The personality results showed an excitable, aggressive and group-orientated personality which made him think that he might find university life confining. The strongest evidence came from his motivational results: the emphasis here was not related to mathematics or science but much more to a job in which he might be involved with organizations. It seemed clear that he had ambitions and wanted a lifestyle that he would not find in a purely academic career.

Looking through the lists of opportunities corresponding to his summary pattern, the idea of marketing appealed strongly. He then reflected that he had once considered studying economics rather than mathematics, and this might have been more relevant to his interest in politics and business. With marketing as a career, he could make use of all his logical and numerical talents but have plenty of chance to draw them out working with others and making decisions in a challenging and varied commercial environment. He decided to go to business school and take a degree in Business Administration. He joined a large company as a graduate trainee gaining general experience until he joined the marketing department. He hopes to become director of marketing of a sizeable company or alternatively run his own business one day.

Case study 4: The reluctant social worker

Marie was a residential social worker at a local school for the physically handicapped. She had worked part time there while still at school and had been offered a job when she left at 16. She did not have enough qualifications to go on to become a qualified social worker. She was now 22 and beginning to think about where her career should go. Although she quite enjoyed life at the school she felt herself getting increasingly irritated by the 'systems'. She also felt that her life generally was not developing; the residential aspect of her life meant that she worked very unsociable hours.

On completing the tests, she obtained the following results:

	least suitable	*most suitable*
Ability	technical	numerical verbal
Personality	group	excitable aggressive
Motivation	literary research	social executive

She did better on the ability tests than she had expected but still not well enough to make further academic study easy. She did best on the numerical and verbal reasoning (she admitted to having quite enjoyed school although she hadn't taken it particularly seriously).

More surprising to Marie were her personality results. She had always seen herself as a group member with a fairly placid approach to life. The results, however, suggested that she was actually excitable and aggressive and this was why she was finding the regimented approach of the school increasingly difficult to cope with. She was not particularly group-orientated although she was by no means a loner. This also fitted in with her feelings of never having a private life.

The pattern suggested that she needed opportunities to initiate activity and be a great deal more directive in her approach. The motivation results suggested that while she enjoyed contact with other people, she also wanted a little more 'business'-type activity in which she could employ a more persuasive approach and see some end results of her labours.

When her results were combined and various opportunities explored it became obvious that Marie was more suited to employment in which she could provide a service to others but have considerably more say, and where her lively and cheerful approach would be of benefit. Some kind of self-employment was also explored. On looking closely at the opportunities available locally, she decided to move into the retail trade, getting a job in a small specialist health food shop (a general interest of hers for some years) where the local owner was looking for a new assistant who could ultimately manage the shop on his behalf.

The change to a retail environment liberated Marie and her friends commented on how much happier she seemed. After six months the shop owner had enough confidence in her approach and knowledge of the products to allow her to manage the shop, with very successful results.

Putting it all together

Summary chart

Write in below the vital descriptions of yourself as they have appeared from the three areas of analysis you have worked through.

	least suitable	*most suitable*
Ability		
Personality		
Motivation		

Myself as I am now

Regarding how successful I feel with my career right now, this is how I would rate myself:

bad ⊢─┼─┼─┼─┼─┼─┼─┤ **wonderful**
    0   1   2   3   4   5   6   7

This is how I look:

_____
_____
_____

This is what I own:

_____
_____
_____

This is how I feel about myself:

_____
_____
_____

People I know say these things about me:

_____
_____
_____

I can describe how I feel about my present occupation using these words:

_____
_____
_____

Possible careers suggested most strongly by my results

Abilities

1. _____

2. _____

3. _____

Personality

1. _____

2. _____

3. _____

Motivation

1. _____

2. _____

3. _____

Overall most suitable career(s) (That/Those which recur(s) most often or with the strongest attraction)

1. _____

2. _____

3. _____

Is there anything which might prevent me from achieving my chosen career?

1. **Health**

_____

_____

2. **Circumstances**

_____

_____

3. **Lack of appropriate education**

_____

_____

4. **Age/experience**

_____

_____

5. **Present commitments**

_____

_____

6. **Risks**

_____

_____

7. **Other**

_____

_____

Preparation
Write a sentence in relation to each of the previous points (1–7)
stating how the things which might prevent you will in fact be
overcome.

1. _____

_____

_____

2. _____

_____

_____

3. _____

_____

_____

4. _____

_____

_____

5. _____

_____

_____

6. _____

_____

_____

7. _____

_____

_____

In order to obtain the career you want, write down first of all the necessary actions to be taken within the next week. Make out a second list for the actions you will have carried out within the next six months.

1. *Next week*

_____

_____

_____

_____

_____

_____

_____

2. *Six months*

_____

_____

_____

_____

_____

_____

Write down the names of the key people who will influence or be affected by your career decisions. Write down as closely and as exactly as you can what they are likely to say.

Name   *What will probably be said*

1. _____   _____

   _____   _____

   _____   _____

2. _____   _____

   _____   _____

   _____   _____

3. _____   _____

   _____   _____

   _____   _____

4. _____   _____

   _____   _____

   _____   _____

5. _____   _____

   _____   _____

   _____   _____

Write down your reaction to what might be said on the previous page.

1. _____

_____

_____

2. _____

_____

_____

3. _____

_____

_____

4. _____

_____

_____

5. _____

_____

_____

Myself in a year's time

Think carefully about how you will be when you have obtained your career objectives or at least worked significantly towards them.

This is how satisfied I feel with my career success:

bad ├───┼───┼───┼───┼───┼───┤ wonderful
    0   1   2   3   4   5   6   7

This is how I shall look:

_____

_____

_____

This is what I shall own:

_____

_____

_____

This is how I shall feel about myself:

_____

_____

_____

People I know will say these things about me:

_____

_____

_____

I will describe my occupation using these words:

_____

_____

_____

Career index

By this stage in the book you should have worked through the various ability tests, personality and motivation measures and have begun to pull all the information together. At each stage we have suggested many illustrative careers; the career index provides a further structured approach to matching your aptitudes with those most usually found in successful members of the career. This process is called 'trait matching'.

The aim is to match a person's individual aptitudes and disposition as closely as possible with those careers most likely to use and encourage them. This will give the individual the most scope for applying his or her skills. It is obvious that some careers demand a particular type of talent, and similarly, a person with a certain kind of personality or motivation may go further in one career than another. The idea of matching is a simple concept, but a great deal of research has been done on the techniques and information upon which it is based.

In a book of this nature, we can only talk about the type of career or broad career area rather than specific posts. Once you have narrowed down your field of search, more detailed advice on specific careers is freely available through the professional bodies, the library services and career advisers.

You should also bear in mind that the nature of what a career actually involves tends to change as the world of work changes.

Success in any job, however, depends first on possessing the appropriate set of basic abilities and then on other factors which are beyond the scope of this book. These could include the difficulty of getting to and from work; how well you get on with your peers and superiors; difficulties in the actual work environment; a certain amount of luck, eg if a position falls vacant at the right time, and so on.

The following list of over 400 careers is not exhaustive but should give you some idea of the range of possibilities.

Using the career index

As you completed the tests and discovered your particular strengths and weaknesses, you will have noticed that each description of a trait was accompanied by some job examples. Most of these examples are to be found in the career index.

When you read the full entries, you will get a clearer picture of which careers are likely to suit you from all directions and which from only one or two directions. You should also look at the level of abilities. In some instances, there will be indicators to suggest that your particular personality or motivation could be a handicap even if you have the correct abilities. This process takes time but eventually you should begin to see which career areas seem most promising. You must then do more individual research, relating specific career requirements or opportunities to your personal circumstances.

Trait matching works because in any identifiable career, there is a type of person who is most usually successful. This is a stereotype. Within any career group, there will be a few people who do not totally conform to the stereotype, but as a general rule, the further you are from the stereotype the more difficult it is to be successful. The idea of this book is for you to follow your aptitudes and find a career which is going to suit you 'naturally', one in which you are most likely to be successful. It does not stop you trying any other career but if your abilities, personality and motivation are not suited to the job, you will have to bring something extra in order to be successful. So collect all your own information together, read the career index carefully, and good hunting!

ABATTOIR WORKER Preferred abilities spatial or technical, and probably a factual personality. Motivation is most likely to be practical.

ACCIDENT ASSESSOR A very specialist role requiring a high level of general ability, an independent personality and motivational factors of an executive and practical nature.

ACCOUNT EXECUTIVE Usually strong verbal or numerical abilities are useful, with an aggressive personality and an executive motivation, sometimes with literary or creative motivation as well.

ACCOUNT PLANNER Numerical and acuity abilities required. Personality is usually passive and motivation is administrative.

ACCOUNTANT Well above average level of ability, particularly in numerical skills; factual and independent personality with administrative motivation. For management roles a more aggressive personality and executive motivation are useful.

ACCOUNTING TECHNICIAN Average to above average abilities, particularly in numerical and acuity; an FCPI personality and administrative motivation.

ACTOR Most levels of ability will find a 'slot' somewhere within the profession but a verbal strength is often helpful; aggressive and independent personality and a creative and literary motivation pattern are also useful, as is the need to combine confidence with sensitivity.

ACTUARY Well above average level of ability particularly numerical, complex and acuity; FCPI personality with administrative motivation.

ACUPUNCTURIST Abilities are most likely to be perceptual or spatial. Personality is calm and feeling. Motivation is social and research.

ADMINISTRATOR Variable level of ability dependent on levels of responsibility, but a joint verbal and numerical pattern required; calm and factual personality with administrative motivation.

ADMISSIONS CLERK Good acuity skills are required, possibly numerical reasoning as well. Coding skills are increasingly desirable. Motivation should be administrative.

ADVERTISING COPYWRITER Verbal abilities; sensitive personality with creative and literary motivational factors, together with considerable ambition in a very competitive environment.

ADVERTISING EXECUTIVE Variable abilities with an FLAG personality and creative and executive motivational factors.

ADVERTISING PHOTOGRAPHER Requires spatial aptitudes. Personality is often excitable and independent. Motivation is creative.

ADVOCATE High-level verbal reasoning and analytical abilities are required. Personality is aggressive. Motivation is literary and/or executive.

AEROBICS INSTRUCTOR Spatial ability is useful. Personality is likely to be excitable and group oriented.

AERODROME CONTROLLER Abilities required are a mixture of numerical, complex, spatial and technical. Personality is often factual and calm. Motivation is likely to be practical, research, possibly an executive interest as well.

AERONAUTICAL ENGINEER Well above average ability with strengths in numerical, complex, spatial and technical; factual, calm, and independent personality with a research and practical motivation pattern.

AERONAUTICAL TECHNICIAN Same characteristics as the aeronautical engineer, but numerical strengths are less required and research interest also less strong.

AEROSPACE SYSTEMS OPERATOR Abilities may be complex reasoning, coding and spatial. Personality most likely to be factual and independent. Likely to have a research motivation.

AGENT (IMPORT/EXPORT) see IMPORT/EXPORT AGENT.

AGENT (MEDIA) Varied aptitudes, an aggressive, usually lively, personality and executive motivation.

AGENT (SALES) Variable abilities and an FLAI personality. Variable motivation factors depending on area of operation, but practical and executive probably most useful.

AGRICULTURAL ENGINEER Above average skills, particularly numeracy, spatial and technical. Motivation is likely to be research and practical.

AGRICULTURAL MECHANIC Average to above average skills, particularly technical and numerical; factual personality with practical motivation and a liking for outdoor activity.

AGRICULTURAL SECRETARY see SECRETARY, but usually mobile.

AGRICULTURALIST Well above average ability, particularly in perceptual and analytical, is usually required for this laboratory-based career; also research and practical motivation. Personality is less precise, but normally factual, calm and independent advisable.

AIR CABIN CREW Variable abilities with an FLPG personality and practical and social motivation.

AIR CONDITIONING MECHANIC Technical aptitudes and a factual, independent personality. Motivation is practical.

AIR GROUND CREW Aptitudes are technical, personality passive and motivation practical.

AIR TRAFFIC CONTROLLER Above average ability with strengths in the spatial and acuity areas; factual and calm personality with administrative motivation.

AIRCRAFT ENGINEER Numerical and spatial skills. Personality is likely to be factual, whilst motivation is research and practical.

AIRLINE PILOT Needs skills of numeracy, spatial and technical skills. Personality is calm and factual. Motivation most likely to be research and executive, but might also be practical.

AIRMAN/WOMAN Technical and spatial aptitudes with a factual and aggressive personality. Motivation practical, but may also include executive.

AIRPORT FIREFIGHTER Technical skills required. Passive and calm personality. Motivation is practical.

AMBULANCE CREW Variable abilities with an FCPG personality and social motivation.

ANAESTHETIST Well above average ability with an analytical and perceptual bias; factual, calm and independent personality with research and administrative motivations.

ANIMAL KEEPER (ZOO or LABORATORY) Average all-round abilities usually with a fairly calm and independent personality and clear practical motivations. Very limited opportunities exist, so persistence is also required.

ANIMAL NURSE see ANIMAL KEEPER, VETERINARY NURSE

ANTHROPOLOGIST Well above average ability of a fairly general nature. Personality will vary according to the particular bias of the work; experimental, academic or literary. Normally more factual, feeling and independent than group-orientation. Literary and research motivations are usual.

ANTIQUE DEALER Variable levels of ability are found, normally with a bias towards numerical and spatial; personality is also variable depending on the type of establishment/practice but within the business field a factual and aggressive approach is valuable, together with practical and some executive interests.

APPLIANCE REPAIRER Technical skills are required. A willingness to work independently is needed, whilst it is necessary to be motivated by practical work.

APPLICATIONS PROGRAMMER Aptitudes may be perceptual, spatial and/or complex, with some coding skill as well. Personality is most likely to be factual and the motivation research and creative.

ARBORIST Above to well above average ability, with a bias on spatial and technical skills; an ECPI personality with practical and research motivation.

ARCHAEOLOGIST Well above average abilities are normally fairly mixed; an independent personality and literary, research motivations needed for positions in a very competitive environment.

ARCHITECT Well above average ability specializing in numerical and spatial areas, with an ELAI personality and creative and practical motivation.

ARCHITECTURAL TECHNICIAN Average to above average ability with a specialization in technical and acuity skills and a calm personality.

ARCHIVIST Well above average ability, with verbal normally a strength. FCPI personality and research and administrative motivation.

ARMED FORCES OFFICER Average to above average ability without any strong specialization; FCAG personality with social and some practical motivation.

ARMED FORCES PERSONNEL All types of ability are required as well as various personality types. Motivation is likely to be practical or administrative for most ranks, though specialist positions often require other interests.

ARMOURER Technical, spatial, numerical abilities with a factual personality. Motivation likely to be directed towards practical and research.

AROMATHERAPIST Perceptual aptitudes are often found. Personality is likely to be feeling, passive and independent. Motivation is likely to be a mixture of research, creative and people.

ART DEALER Numerical and spatial abilities, usually with a factual and independent personality and creative, executive motivations.

ART EDITOR Spatial aptitudes and a feeling personality. Requires creative motivation.

ART GALLERY CURATOR/KEEPER Verbal, perceptual and spatial aptitudes are often required. Acuity is often essential as well. Personality is likely to be feeling, passive and independent, whilst motivation will lean towards literary, creative and research activities – all the intellectual ones, in other words!

ART RESTORER Spatial aptitudes are likely to be required. Personality is likely to be feeling, passive and independent, whilst motivation is creative.

ART THERAPIST Above average general abilities with spatial specialization; a feeling, calm personality (often independent) with social and creative motivation.

ARTIFICER Numerical, technical, spatial, coding and perceptual aptitudes are all required in these complicated technical jobs. Personality is likely to be factual and calm. Motivation is likely to be research and practical.

ARTIST Average to above average ability for professional training and with definite feeling, independent personality factors, creative motivation.

ARTS ADMINISTRATOR Aptitudes required are likely to be a mixture of verbal, numerical, perceptual, acuity and coding. Personality is most likely to be calm. Motivation will be administrative, but may also include executive and creative.

ASSEMBLY WORKER Technical and spatial aptitudes are most useful together with a practical motivation.

ASTRONAUT Aptitudes are likely to be broad including numerical, perceptual, complex, spatial, technical and coding. Personality is likely to be factual, calm, whilst motivation is most likely to be research.

ASTRONOMER Well above average complex, numerical and perceptual abilities; factual and calm, independent personality with strong research motivation.

AUCTIONEER Variable abilities; FLAG personality and executive and practical motivation. The higher levels of ability are needed for professional qualifications.

AUDIOLOGY TECHNICIAN Above average ability, particularly numerical and technical; variable personality but usually factual and calm with practical and some research motivation.

AUDITOR Well above average ability, particularly numerical and analytical; with an FCPI personality and administrative motivation.

AUTHOR Variable abilities, an ELAI personality and literary motivation.

AUTOMOBILE DESIGNER Numerical, technical and spatial aptitudes are required at a high level. Motivation is likely to be creative and research.

AUTOMOBILE TECHNICIAN Technical and/or spatial aptitudes are required. Motivation is practical.

AVIONICS ENGINEER Numerical, complex, spatial, technical and coding aptitudes are all required. Personality is most likely to be factual. Motivation is likely to be towards research or research and practical.

BACTERIOLOGIST Well above average ability, particularly perceptual and analytical; passive, factual and often independent personality with research and some practical motivation.

BAGGAGE HANDLER Spatial or technical aptitudes are useful, with a practical motivation.

BAKER Technical and some perceptual ability, often with an independent and calm personality and practical motivation.

BALLET DANCER Variable abilities; ELAI personality and creative motivation, plus a great deal of hard work in the formative years.

BANDSPERSON Most likely to have a feeling personality and a creative motivation.

BANK CLERK Above average ability, particularly in acuity and numerical skills; usually factual, passive and independent personality with administrative motivation.

BANK MANAGER Above average ability, with numerical and acuity uppermost; FCAG personality, administrative and executive motivation.

BAR PERSON Variable abilities; FLPG personality.

BARRISTER Above average verbal ability with some analytical; FCAI personality with literary and administrative motivation.

BEAUTICIAN Average ability, often with spatial and acuity strengths. An ELAG personality with creative and research motivation.

BESPOKE TAILOR Spatial aptitudes required. Motivation most likely to be creative, but could also have an executive element.

BICYCLE REPAIRER Technical aptitudes together with a practical motivation. A career on the retail side will require some executive motivation as well.

BILINGUAL SECRETARY Above average verbal ability and literary motivation. Personality will vary with the type of environment in which the secretary operates.

BIOLOGIST Well above average abilities, particularly perceptual and analytical; passive, factual and often independent personality in research and some practical and research motivation.

BIOMEDICAL ENGINEER Well above average ability, with particular strengths in perceptual, spatial, technical. Variable personality depending on employment environment, with research and practical motivation.

BLACKSMITH/FARRIER Technical ability with factual and independent personality, often with an aggressive but calm approach; practical motivation.

BOAT BUILDER   Variable abilities and personality but strongly practical motivation.

BOOKBINDER   Spatial and technical abilities together with a passive and independent personality and a creative and practical motivation.

BOOK CRITIC   High verbal abilities with aggressive and independent personality and literary motivation.

BOOK EDITOR   Verbal and acuity aptitudes are required, though sometimes perceptual aptitudes also reveal a talent for this work. Personality is likely to be passive and independent. Motivation is most likely to be literary and/or creative.

BOOK ILLUSTRATOR   Perceptual and spatial abilities; usually a feeling and independent personality with creative motivation.

BOOK PUBLISHER   Aptitudes may be verbal, complex and analytical. Personality is likely to be aggressive. Motivation will be executive, possibly also with creative and/or literary.

BOOKKEEPER   Numerical and acuity abilities; factual and passive personality and administrative motivation.

BOOKMAKER   *see* TURF ACCOUNTANT.

BOOKSELLER   Variable abilities but often high verbal and a clearly independent and often excitable personality; executive and administrative motivation.

BOOM OPERATOR   Technical or spatial aptitudes are useful. Motivation is likely to be practical and creative.

BOTANIST   Well above average perceptual abilities; independent, passive personality and research interests for this usually laboratory-based area.

BREWER   Perceptual and technical abilities, usually with a fairly independent personality and practical, research motivation.

BRICKLAYER   Variable abilities but often technical skills, with a fairly aggressive and independent personality and highly practical motivation.

BROKER   Above average numerical and analytical abilities; factual, aggressive personality with executive, administrative motivation and flair!

BUILDER'S MERCHANT Variable abilities and personality (often aggressive) with practical, administrative motivation.

BUILDING DEMOLITION EXPERT Requires technical aptitudes, a factual, calm personality and practical motivation.

BUILDING INSPECTOR Above average perceptual and technical abilities; factual, aggressive and independent personality and practical and administrative motivation.

BUILDING OPERATIVE Spatial or technical aptitudes most useful. A factual personality is normally found together with practical motivation.

BUILDING SOCIETY MANAGER/ASSISTANT Above average numerical and acuity abilities, variable personality and administrative motivation.

BURSAR Well above average numerical and acuity abilities; variable personality depending on employment area with administrative and sometimes executive motivations. Usually requires a specialist accounting qualification.

BUS CONDUCTOR Variable abilities with an FLPI and social and practical motivations.

BUS DRIVER Variable abilities, strongly independent personality and practical motivation.

BUSINESS CONSULTANT Above average ability with particular strengths in numerical and verbal; ECAI personality with executive motivation.

BUSINESS MACHINE SERVICE ENGINEER Technical aptitudes and a factual, independent personality as well as practical motivation.

BUTCHER Variable abilities but often spatial strength; frequently an independent personality with practical motivation.

BUYER Average to above average numerical abilities, often with a spatial and technical supporting strength. An FLAI personality with creative and executive motivation.

CABARET PERFORMER Personality is likely to be feeling, excitable and independent, whilst creative motivation is required.

CABINET MAKER Variable abilities (bias towards spatial and technical) and variable personality depending on employment environment, strongly creative and practical motivation.

CAMERA OPERATOR Above average technical ability with factual and calm personality; creative and practical motivations.

CAMERA REPAIRER Perceptual, spatial and technical aptitudes are required. Personality is likely to be factual, calm, passive and independent. Motivation is likely to be creative with also research and/or practical.

CANINE BEAUTICIAN Spatial aptitudes are useful. Motivation may be creative or practical with some executive interest for running a business.

CANTEEN COUNTER ASSISTANT All types of aptitude whilst personality is likely to be passive. Motivation is most likely to be social or practical.

CAR BODY DESIGNER Spatial aptitudes with creative motivation.

CAR MECHANIC Technical aptitudes with practical motivation.

CARDIOLOGY TECHNICIAN Aptitudes most likely to be perceptual or spatial with a factual, passive and independent personality. Research and people motivation likely to be paramount.

CARE ASSISTANT Feeling, calm and group-oriented personality with a people motivation.

CAREERS ADVISER Above average general ability, calm and independent personality and social motivations.

CARPENTER Variable abilities, but often with bias towards spatial and technical areas and strongly practical motivation. Personality will vary according to the employment environment.

CARPET FITTER Spatial aptitudes required with practical motivation. Independent personality is usually helpful in this work.

CARTOGRAPHER Well above average ability (particularly spatial) and some numerical skills, with a factual, independent and usually calm personality and creative and research motivations.

CARTOON ANIMATOR Spatial aptitudes, feeling personality and creative motivation are the most likely mixture of talents for this very specialized, innovative work.

CASHIER Often above average ability, particularly in acuity and/or numerical areas, usually fairly passive, group personality with administrative motivation.

CD-ROM PRODUCER Personality is likely to be factual and aggressive. Motivation may be executive and perhaps creative or research. Aptitudes are likely to be numerical.

CHAPLAIN Motivation is social whilst personality is feeling.

CHAUFFEUR/CHAUFFEUSE An independent, passive personality is most likely to be suited to this work. Motivation is likely to be practical.

CHEF/COOK Variable abilities, often with spatial strengths; FLPI personality and practical, creative and administrative motivation, together with the ability to work unsociable hours.

CHEMICAL ENGINEER see TECHNOLOGIST.

CHEMICAL PLANT PROCESS WORKER Technical and spatial aptitudes are required. A factual, calm personality is useful as well as practical motivation.

CHEMICAL TECHNICIAN Perceptual and numerical aptitudes, as well as a factual personality are required. Motivation is towards research and perhaps practical.

CHEMICAL TECHNOLOGIST Aptitudes are numerical, perceptual and complex. Personality is factual and motivation is research.

CHEMIST Well above average perceptual and analytical abilities combined with research motivation.

CHIEF EXECUTIVE Verbal, numerical and analytical aptitudes are all required in varying measures. Complex aptitudes are often useful as well. Personality is aggressive, whilst motivation is executive, often with administrative as a secondary interest.

CHILD CARE WORKER A feeling personality with a people motivation is required.

CHILDREN'S NURSE Aptitudes are most likely to be perceptual, personality calm and passive, whilst there may well be motivation towards people and research.

CHIMNEY SWEEP Variable abilities with an increasingly technical bias; FLPI personality and practical motivation.

CHIROPODIST Above average general ability, calm and independent personality with social motivation.

CHOREOGRAPHER Variable ability and personality is often feeling and excitable, with a creative and administrative motivation and considerable determination.

CINEMA MANAGER Variable abilities, with numerical and acuity skills often predominating, a balanced personality (but often independent and sometimes aggressive) with creative and adminsitrative motivation.

CIVIL ENGINEER Well above average abilities, particularly in complex, numerical and technical areas with a factual, independent personality, often with some aggressive tendencies, and practical and executive motivations.

CIVIL ENGINEERING OPERATIVE Technical, spatial aptitudes together with a factual personality and practical motivation.

CIVIL SERVANT Variable levels of ability, depending on the level of aspiration; personality will vary with the various departments and working environments but frequently factual, passive and group factors predominate, together with strong administrative motivation.

CLERK Acuity abilities predominate, with administrative interests, but personality varying with the employment environment.

CLINICAL PSYCHOLOGIST Well above average ability, frequently with perceptual and analytical strengths. Factual, calm and independent personality most usual, together with social and research motivation.

CLOTH CUTTER Spatial aptitudes are required.

CLOTHING DESIGNER Spatial aptitudes, creative motivation with an independent, feeling personality are important elements.

CLOTHING PRESSER Practical motivation most relevant.

CLOWN Feeling and excitable personality probably the most appropriate together with creative motivation.

CLUB MANAGER Variable abilities with an FLAG personality and executive and administrative motivation.

COACH DRIVER Motivation required is most obviously practical.

COASTGUARD Variable abilities with a factual and independent personality and practical interests; follows a sea-going first career.

COMIC ILLUSTRATOR Spatial aptitudes usually reveal this talent, though it might also be revealed on the perceptual test. Motivation is creative.

COMMUNITY SOCIAL WORKER Very similar to community warden, but with more variety in personality and at the social activity level.

COMMUNITY WARDEN Variable abilities, an ECPG personality, with social and practical motivation.

COMPANY SECRETARY Well above average ability, with particular verbal and numerical strengths; factual, calm and independent personality with a literary and administrative motivation.

COMPOSITOR Spatial and technical abilities, a factual, calm personality and literary and practical motivation.

COMPUTER ANIMATOR Spatial aptitudes, independent personality and creative motivation.

COMPUTER ENGINEER Well above average numerical, technical and analytical abilities; factual, calm and independent personality with research and practical motivation.

COMPUTER GAME DESIGNER Numerical, complex, coding aptitudes. Independent personality. Creative and research motivation.

COMPUTER OPERATOR Variable abilities with strong acuity and/or coding skills and a passive personality with administrative interests.

COMPUTER PROGRAMMER Above average analytical abilities, a factual and independent personality, with research and administrative motivation.

COMPUTER SYSTEMS ANALYST Numerical, complex, spatial and coding aptitudes are all important. Factual and independent personality with research motivation.

COMPUTER TECHNICIAN Technical and spatial aptitudes are important. Personality is likely to be factual, whilst motivation most likely to be practical.

CONFECTIONER Variable abilities with a useful bias towards the perceptual; creative and practical motivation. Personality varies according to the type of employment organization.

CONFERENCE EXECUTIVE Verbal, numerical and acuity abilities; factual, calm and frequently independent personality, with literary, executive motivation.

CONSERVATION OFFICER Independent, calm personality with practical or research motivation.

CONSTRUCTION OPERATIVE Spatial and technical abilities are useful. Personality is most likely to be factual, whilst motivation is practical.

CONSTRUCTION PLANT OPERATOR Technical aptitudes are useful. Factual, independent personality, with a practical motivation.

CONSUMER RESEARCH EXECUTIVE Acuity and/or coding skills appropriate. Motivation is administrative, sometimes executive.

CONTINUITY SUPERVISOR Analytical, perceptual and spatial aptitudes may all be important. Personality is usually feeling, group oriented and excitable, whilst motivation is creative or literary.

COPYWRITER Strong verbal ability with independent personality and literary motivation.

CORONER Aptitudes would include numerical, perceptual, complex, but could include other visual and technical ones as well. Personality is likely to be factual and calm. Motivation is most likely to be research.

COST ACCOUNTANT Above average numerical ability with factual, calm personality and administrative motivation.

COSTUME DESIGNER Spatial aptitudes, a feeling personality and creative motivation are the elements most likely to lead to success in this work.

COUNSELLOR Aptitudes are likely to contain high verbal, analytical, complex or perceptual elements. A feeling, independent and calm personality is helpful. Motivation will be social.

COUNTER SERVICE ASSISTANT A mixture of acuity, coding and spatial abilities would be useful. Personality may be passive whilst motivation is most likely to be administrative.

COUNTRYSIDE RANGER/WARDEN Technical or spatial aptitudes are useful. Personality is likely to be calm and independent. Motivation will show a strong leaning to the practical.

COURIER Variable abilities, aggressive and independent personality, social and administrative motivation.

COURT REPORTER Acuity and verbal skills are required. An independent personality may help to be successful in this work, whilst motivation may well be literary.

COURT USHER/OFFICER A calm and passive personality could be useful, probably with literary, social or administrative motivation.

CRANE OPERATOR Technical and spatial aptitudes are most desirable. Personality may well be factual, calm, passive and independent. It would be difficult to sustain interest in this work without practical motivation.

CRIMINOLOGIST Aptitudes are likely to be high and could well be a mixture of analytical, perceptual and complex. A calm and independent personality is most likely together with a research motivation.

CRUISE DIRECTOR An aggressive, excitable and group personality helps with this career. Executive, creative and administrative motivation are all relevant.

CRYPTOGRAPHER Demands of this type of work are likely to include complex, analytical and coding aptitudes. Personality is likely to be calm and factual. Research is likely to be the strongest motivation.

CULTURAL ANTHROPOLOGIST Verbal and perceptual aptitudes may feature at a high level. Personality most likely to be feeling and independent, Motivation could contain elements of literary, creative and research.

CURATOR Above average ability; ECPI personality with creative and research motivation.

CURRENCY TRADER Numerical and acuity aptitudes are likely to be seen. A factual, excitable, aggressive personality will often help with success in this work, as well as executive motivation.

CUSTOMER SERVICES MANAGER Acuity aptitudes are helpful as is a factual personality and an administrative motivation.

CUSTOMS OFFICER Above average general abilities (with strong numerical skills if in the VAT section); FCAI personality and practical and administrative motivation.

DANCE INSTRUCTOR Same as the dancer (below) but may also have social motivation.

DANCER Various abilities with an ELAI personality and creative motivation.

DATABASE ADMINISTRATOR Numerical, complex and coding aptitudes. Factual, independent personality. Research motivation, sometimes with administrative and/or creative.

DEAF INTERPRETER Personality is likely to be feeling and passive, whilst motivation is likely to be social.

DECK OFFICER Numerical, spatial aptitudes are likely to feature. A factual, calm personality goes well with this work as does a practical motivation.

DECK RATING Technical aptitudes are useful. A factual, calm personality is likely to be evident with a practical motivation.

DECORATOR Technical and spatial abilities with an FLPI personality and practical motivation.

DELIVERY VAN DRIVER Practical motivation most important.

DEMONSTRATOR Technical and spatial abilities with an ELAG personality and executive, practical motivation.

DENTAL ASSISTANT General abilities, often with spatial and acuity strengths; FLPG personality and social and practical motivation.

DENTAL HYGIENIST Above average spatial and technical abilities; factual, excitable and often group personality with social and practical motivation.

DENTAL NURSE see NURSE, but with more 'office' hours.

DENTAL TECHNICIAN Technical ability with a factual, calm personality and practical motivation.

DENTIST Well above average spatial and technical abilities; an FCAI personality, with social and research motivation.

DERMATOLOGIST Perceptual aptitudes can be important together with a factual, independent personality and research motivation.

DERRICKMAN A factual personality is useful together with practical motivation.

DESIGN ENGINEER Numerical and spatial abilities to well above average level, with variable personality depending on employment organization and a creative and practical motivation.

DESIGNER Above average ability, frequently with spatial skills, an independent, feeling personality and creative motivation.

DIETICIAN Well above average ability, often with perceptual and analytical strengths: FLPI personality and research motivation.

DIPLOMATIC SERVICE STAFF Acuity, coding and verbal aptitudes are important. Personality varies widely with the nature of the specific role. Motivation is most often administrative and executive.

DIRECTOR (MEDIA) Variable abilities, often feeling and independent personality and creative and executive motivation.

DISC JOCKEY Variable abilities, with an ELPI personality and social and practical motivation.

DISPENSING OPTICIAN Above average perceptual and spatial abilities, often with acuity skills; a calm and independent personality and executive and research motivation.

DISPENSING PHARMACIST Very similar to dispensing optician.

DISPLAY ARTIST Spatial ability; often feeling, excitable, independent personality and creative and practical motivation.

DISTRICT NURSE Similar to midwife.

DIVER Technical ability, with an FCPI personality and practical motivation.

DOCTOR Well above average numerical, perceptual and analytical abilities; FCAG personality and social motivation.

DOG HANDLER Independent personality and practical motivation required.

DOG TRAINER see DOG HANDLER.

DRAMA TEACHER Verbal and sometimes perceptual abilities are evident, with feeling, excitable personality, as well as literary, creative and social motivation.

DRAUGHTSPERSON Above average numerical, spatial and acuity abilities with a calm and factual personality and creative and research motivation.

DRESSER (STAGE) Variable abilities; calm, feeling, personality with creative and practical motivation.

DRESSMAKER Spatial ability; ECPI personality and creative motivation.

DRILLER Technical aptitudes most useful, as well as factual, independent personality and practical motivation.

DRIVER Variable abilities with an FCPI personality and practical motivation.

DRIVING INSTRUCTOR Possibly more executive motivation than a driver (see above) especially when running a business.

DRUG AND ALCOHOL COUNSELLOR A calm, passive personality may be most likely to suit this vocation, whilst social motivation will be required.

DRY CLEANER Practical motivation is necessary.

DYEING TECHNICIAN Perceptual aptitudes are likely to be required, together with a factual personality and research motivation.

ECOLOGIST High perceptual aptitudes, an independent personality and research motivation are the elements likely to required in this specialized branch of science.

ECONOMIST Well above average verbal and numerical abilities, research motivation and a variable personality depending on working environment.

EDITOR (FILM) Perceptual, coding and spatial aptitudes are all important. Personality is likely to be passive and independent, whilst motivation is creative.

EDITOR (NEWSPAPER) Verbal and spatial abilities with an independent and aggressive personality and literary and executive motivation.

EDITORIAL CARTOONIST A feeling, independent personality is most likely to be associated with this unusual, individual work, though there cannot possibly be any hard rules about this type of talent and inclination, though motivation is creative or literary.

EDUCATION OFFICER Numerical, perceptual and acuity aptitudes are required. Personality is likely to be calm and passive, whilst motivation is mainly administrative.

EDUCATIONAL PSYCHOLOGIST Well above average ability; calm, independent personality and creative and research motivation, together with teaching qualification and experience with disturbed children.

ELECTRICAL ENGINEER Above average spatial and technical abilities and research and practical motivation. Personality more variable, but frequently factual and independent.

ELECTRICIAN Technical ability and variable personality with practical motivation.

ELECTRONICS ENGINEER Aptitudes may be complex, numerical and sometimes spatial as well. Personality is factual and motivation is research.

ELEMENTARY SCHOOL TEACHER Aptitudes may be varied. Personality most likely to be passive and group oriented. Motivation needs to be social, but may also show literary or creative elements.

EMBALMER Variable abilities; factual, calm, passive personality with creative and practical motivation.

EMPLOYMENT OFFICER Above average general ability, usually with a calm, factual personality and social and administrative motivation.

ENGINEER Numerical aptitudes with either spatial or technical or both. Coding may also appear. Personality is factual though there are many differences within the field of engineering. Motivation is usually research and practical, but again depends upon specialized branch of engineering.

ENGINEERING OFFICER Numerical, spatial and technical aptitudes need to be strong. Personality is likely to be factual and calm. Motivation is most likely to be practical, but could also show some administrative interest.

ENGINEERING PATTERN MAKER Spatial and technical abilities with a creative, practical motivation. Personality more variable, depending on employment environment.

ENGINEERING TECHNICAL AUTHOR Verbal and analytical aptitudes may appear as strongly as numerical, perceptual, technical or spatial ones. Personality is likely to be independent. Motivation may combine literary with research.

ENGINEERING TECHNICIAN Above average numerical and technical abilities, with factual and independent personality and practical motivation.

ENGLISH LANGUAGE TEACHER Verbal and analytical aptitudes together with a feeling personality as well as literary, and possibly also social, motivation.

ENGRAVER Technical and spatial abilities; passive and independent personality and creative and practical motivation.

ENTERTAINMENTS OFFICER Variable abilities, with a group-orientated and aggressive personality and literary and administrative motivation.

ENVIRONMENTAL HEALTH OFFICER Well above average ability, frequently with perceptual and analytical strengths; a factual and independent personality and research and practical motivation.

EQUESTRIAN No specific aptitudes though obviously skills of dexterity and balance are essential. Similarly, personality may be of different types. A practical motivation is certainly required.

ERGONOMIST Well above average spatial and analytical abilities, with a calm and often independent personality and research and practical motivation.

ESTATE AGENT Variable abilities, FLAG personality and executive and practical motivation.

ESTATE MANAGER Variable abilities (but increasingly professionally qualified), with a factual, calm and often aggressive personality and executive and administrative motivation.

ESTIMATOR Numerical, spatial and acuity aptitudes are appropriate. Personality is factual and sometimes independent. Motivation is administrative, but can also be practical.

EXHAUST/TYRE FITTER Technical aptitude, a factual personality and practical motivation are required.

EXHIBITION ORGANIZER *see* CONFERENCE EXECUTIVE.

EXPLOSIVES EXPERT Spatial and technical aptitudes need to be strong. Complex aptitudes can also reveal a talent for this type of work. A factual, calm personality is required together with practical motivation although some research motivation may also appear.

FABRICATION ENGINEER Spatial and technical aptitudes are important, together with a factual personality and practical motivation.

FACTORY INSPECTOR Spatial, technical aptitudes and a factual, calm personality with practical motivation, sometimes administrative motivation as well.

FARMER Above average ability, particularly in perceptual or technical areas, frequently factual, aggressive and independent personality and practical motivation.

FARM MANAGER As for farmer, but with additional executive motivation.

FARM SECRETARY Verbal, numerical and acuity abilities with an FCPG personality and practical and administrative motivation.

FARM WORKER Technical aptitudes are required, a calm, passive, independent personality and practical motivation.

FASHION BUYER Variable abilities, usually with spatial skills, with an independent and aggressive (frequently excitable) personality and creative and executive motivation.

FASHION DESIGNER Spatial ability; excitable, aggressive and independent personality with creative and practical motivation.

FASHION MODEL Spatial aptitudes are helpful in this type of work. Personality is likely to be feeling, excitable and passive. Creative motivation required.

FAST FOOD COUNTER ASSISTANT/MANAGER No specific aptitudes required. A manager is likely to be more aggressive. Motivation is practical, though a manager may have more executive motivation.

FILM CAMERA OPERATOR Spatial or perceptual aptitudes are needed, whilst technical ones are also useful. An independent, calm and passive personality with creative motivation.

FILM PROJECTIONIST Technical ability with an independent and calm personality; creative and practical motivation.

FILM REVIEWER Verbal ability; independent personality and creative and literary motivation.

FINANCIAL ANALYST Above average numerical and analytical abilities with executive and administrative motivation but more variable personality, depending on working environment.

FINANCIAL CONTROLLER Numerical and acuity ability; factual, calm and aggressive personality and administrative motivation.

FIREFIGHTER Variable abilities; an FCPG personality and practical motivation.

FISH FARM WORKER Factual and independent personality and practical motivation.

FISHERIES OFFICER Acuity skills, factual personality and administrative, practical motivation.

FISHERMAN Variable abilities with a factual and often passive personality and practical motivation.

FITTER Technical ability and practical motivation, with variable but usually factual personality.

FLIGHT ATTENDANT Acuity skills often required. A passive personality with social and practical motivation.

FLOOR LAYER Spatial aptitudes required. A factual, independent personality and practical motivation.

FLORIST Spatial ability and feeling and independent personality with creative motivation.

FLYMAN (THEATRE) Variable abilities; calm and independent personality and creative and practical motivation.

FOOD HYGIENE INSPECTOR Perceptual, acuity and coding abilities. A factual, calm and independent personality. Practical and research motivation.

FOOD SCIENTIST Numerical and perceptual aptitudes, a factual personality and research motivation.

FOOD SERVICE WORKER No special aptitudes required. Personality most likely to be passive, whilst motivation is practical.

FOREIGN CORRESPONDENT Verbal and analytical aptitudes at a high level. An aggressive, independent personality often goes well with this work, as does a creative and literary motivation.

FOREIGN LANGUAGE TEACHER Verbal abilities are required. Personality most likely to be feeling, excitable and passive. Motivation is usually creative and literary.

FORENSIC SCIENTIST (eg pathologist, psychologist) Well above average complex, perceptual and analytical abilities with a factual, calm and independent personality and research motivation.

FORESTER Technical ability, strong independent personality, frequently calm; factual and practical motivation with a preference for the outdoor life.

FOUNDRY WORKER Spatial and technical aptitudes. A factual, calm personality and practical motivation.

FRANCHISE OPERATOR Acuity skills are required as well as other abilities depending upon the nature of the franchise. Personality is likely to be aggressive and the motivation executive.

FREELANCE WRITER Verbal aptitudes and an independent personality together with a literary motivation.

FRENCH POLISHER Spatial aptitudes together with a creative, practical motivation are required.

FUND RAISER Acuity and numerical skills required together with an aggressive personality and executive, administrative motivation.

FUNERAL DIRECTOR Technical and acuity abilities; calm and independent personality with a balanced factual/feeling score and social and executive motivation.

FURNITURE MAKER Spatial and technical abilities, often with an independent, calm personality and practical motivation.

GAMEKEEPER Variable abilities and passive and independent personality; practical motivation; prepared to be isolated and out in all weathers.

GARDENER Variable abilities but a technical strength often helps; an ECPI personality with creative and practical motivation.

GARMENT EXAMINER Spatial aptitudes are useful. Personality often creative.

GENEALOGIST Above average verbal and analytical abilities; factual and independent personality and research and literary motivation.

GENETICIST Well above average perceptual and analytical abilities and research motivation. Personality variable but often factual and independent.

GEOCHEMIST Well above average perceptual and analytical abilities with factual, often independent, personality and research and practical motivation.

GEOLOGIST see GEOCHEMIST.

GEOPHYSICIST see GEOCHEMIST.

GLASS BLOWER Spatial aptitudes, a feeling, independent personality and creative motivation.

GLAZIER Technical ability with an often factual and independent personality and practical motivation.

GOLDSMITH Spatial and technical abilities, often passive and independent personality and creative motivation.

GOLF PROFESSIONAL Spatial aptitudes often strong. A factual, aggressive personality together with executive, practical motivation.

GRAPHIC DESIGNER Spatial and acuity abilities and creative motivation. Personality more variable, but often feeling and independent.

GREEN KEEPER Spatial aptitudes, a calm and passive personality and practical motivation.

GROCER Variable abilities; factual, excitable and group-orientated personality with practical and administrative motivation.

GROOM No specific aptitudes, but an independent, passive personality as well as practical motivation.

GROUNDSPERSON Variable abilities but often technical strengths; ECPI personality with practical motivation.

GUARD Variable abilities with an FCPG personality and practical abilities.

GUNSMITH Technical ability, often passive and independent personality and practical motivation.

HAIRDRESSER Spatial ability with an FLPG personality and social and practical motivation.

HEAD TEACHER Verbal and numerical abilities (usually above average) and social and executive motivation. Personality tends to be more balanced than clearly defined.

HEALTH AND SAFETY INSPECTOR Perceptual aptitudes, though others may appear. A factual, calm personality and practical motivation.

HEALTH SERVICE ADMINISTRATOR Numerical and acuity aptitudes. A calm, passive personality and administrative motivation.

HEALTH VISITOR Above average ability; calm, independent personality and social motivation.

HEATING ENGINEER Perceptual and technical abilities (above average for professional qualification); factual and independent personality and practical motivation.

HEAVY GOODS VEHICLE DRIVER Aptitudes likely to be more on the visual, technical side than leaning towards words or numbers. Calm, passive, independent personality as well as practical motivation.

HELICOPTER PILOT Numerical, spatial, technical aptitudes need to be strong. Personality is factual and calm. Practical motivation is likely.

HERBALIST Perceptual aptitudes may arise strongly. Personality is feeling and passive whilst motivation may be creative and research.

HISTORIAN Above average acuity and analytical abilities with a passive and factual personality and literary motivation.

HOME ECONOMIST Perceptual aptitudes often accompany this career. Personality tends to be on the factual side whilst motivation is creative.

HOMEOPATH Aptitudes may vary, but perceptual most likely, passive personality and creative as well as research motivation.

HOROLOGIST Technical ability; frequently calm and independent personality with practical motivation.

HORSE RIDING INSTRUCTOR Varied aptitudes, a personality that is independent and tends to be aggressive, with practical motivation.

HORTICULTURALIST Perceptual aptitudes, an independent, passive personality with creative and practical motivation.

HOSPITAL PHYSICIST Above average perceptual and technical abilities with a factual, calm and often independent personality and social and practical motivation.

HOSPITAL PORTER Variable abilities; ECPG personality and social and practical motivation.

HOSTEL WARDEN Variable abilities, calm and factual personality with social and often practical motivation.

HOTEL MANAGER Variable abilities; but strengths in verbal and numerical areas helpful; FLAG personality and social and executive motivation.

HOUSE PARENT Variable abilities; FLPG personality, social and practical motivation.

HOUSING MANAGER Above average ability; factual, calm and independent personality (but not passive) and social and administrative motivation.

HUMAN RESOURCES CONSULTANT/DIRECTOR see PERSONNEL DIRECTOR.

HYDROGRAPHIC SURVEYOR Above average spatial and technical abilities; factual and independent personality with practical and administrative motivation.

HYDROLOGIST Well above average ability, especially in the perceptual and analytical areas with factual and frequently independent personality and a research and practical motivation.

ILLUSTRATOR Varied abilities, but often spatial skills; feeling and passive personality with creative motivation.

IMMUNOLOGIST Numerical, perceptual and coding abilities are all strong. A factual, calm personality with research motivation.

IMPORT/EXPORT AGENT Variable abilities, but numerical and acuity skills useful; FLAI personality and executive motivation.

INDUSTRIAL DESIGNER Spatial and technical abilities with a varying personality, depending on the particular working environment; creative motivation.

INDUSTRIAL NURSE Above average ability, with a calm and reasonably factual personality and social and practical motivation.

INDUSTRIAL RELATIONS OFFICER Variable abilities, usually factual, independent and calm personality and social and administrative motivation.

INDUSTRIAL SAFETY OFFICER Variable abilities, factual and independent personality (usually more aggressive than passive) with practical and administrative motivation.

INFORMATION OFFICER Verbal, analytical and acuity abilities. Personality varies, tending to be group oriented, motivation being literary, but also some interest in executive or administrative.

INFORMATION SCIENTIST Well above average level of ability (frequently technical, coding and analytical strengths); calm, independent and passive personality and literary and research motivation.

INSTRUMENT AND CONTROL ENGINEER Above average ability, often numerical, coding, technical and analytical skills. Variable personality, depending on the working environment, but usually factual and independent with practical and research motivation.

INSTRUMENT MAKER Numerical and technical abilities, often a factual and independent personality with practical motivation.

INSURANCE ADJUSTER Numerical and acuity skills. A factual, calm personality. Motivation administrative.

INSURANCE AGENT Variable abilities but often numerical and verbal skills; an independent, passive and factual personality with executive and administrative motivation.

INTERIOR DESIGNER Variable abilities (often spatial strengths), an ELAI personality and creative motivation.

INTERPRETER Well above average verbal ability with an FLPI personality and literary motivation.

INTERVIEWER Verbal abilities with a group-orientated and often excitable personality and literary and social motivation.

INVESTMENT ADVISOR Analytical, verbal and numerical aptitudes. Personality is factual and aggressive, whilst motivation is executive.

IRONMONGER Variable abilities (numerical and technical are useful); often factual, lively and independent personality and executive and practical motivation.

JEWELLERY MAKER Spatial and acuity abilities with a passive and calm personality; creative, practical motivation.

JOCKEY Aptitudes vary. Usually a factual and aggressive personality with practical motivation.

JOINER Technical ability and practical motivation, but personality would vary according to the kind of working environment.

JOURNALIST Verbal ability with either an ELAG or ECAI personality (depending on the amount of contact with other people expected in the everyday work environment); literary motivation necessary.

JUDGE Verbal, analytical and complex aptitudes. Calm and aggressive personality. Literary motivation appears strongly.

JUSTICE'S CLERK Verbal and acuity abilities (usually above average) with a factual, calm and independent personality and administrative motivation.

KENNEL WORKER Variable abilities with passive, independent personality and practical motivation.

KITCHEN ASSISTANT Variable abilities with a personality tending towards the passive and practical motivation.

LABORATORY TECHNICIAN Above average ability (particularly in analytical and perceptual areas) with technical skills for some laboratories. Personality will be variable, but usually factual and passive with strong research motivation.

LANDSCAPE ARCHITECT Above average ability, particularly spatial, with an independent and aggressive personality and practical and creative motivation.

LANGUAGE TEACHER Above average ability; often factual and aggressive personality with literary and social motivation.

LATHE OPERATOR Spatial aptitudes, sometimes technical. Personality tends to be passive and independent. Motivation is creative/practical.

LAWYER Verbal, analytical aptitudes, often complex as well. Personality aggressive for most work. Motivation a mixture of literary and executive, sometimes administrative.

LEGAL EXECUTIVE Above average verbal, numerical and acuity abilities. Often factual and slightly aggressive personality with literary and administrative motivation.

LEISURE CENTRE STAFF Variable abilities and usually an excitable and independent personality with practical and administrative motivation.

LIBERAL STUDIES TEACHER Above average verbal ability, ELAG personality and social and literary motivation.

LIBRARIAN Well above average verbal ability; ECAI personality and literary motivation.

LIBRARY ASSISTANT Above average verbal ability, an ECPI personality and literary and administrative motivation.

LICENSEE Aptitudes vary. Personality usually factual and fairly aggressive. Personality practical and perhaps executive.

LIGHTHOUSE KEEPER Variable abilities but technical and acuity skills both help. ECPI personality and practical motivation with low social scores. (The job is being phased out by new technology.)

LIGHTING TECHNICIAN (THEATRE) Above average technical ability with a calm and independent personality and creative, practical motivation.

LINGUIST Well above average verbal ability with literary motivation, but personality more variable depending on the working environment.

LITERARY AGENT Verbal ability; calm, independent and practical personality with literary and executive motivation.

LITERARY CRITIC Verbal ability, independent and sensitive personality and literary motivation.

LOCK KEEPER Variable abilities, often factual, calm and independent personality with practical motivation.

LOCKSMITH Spatial and technical abilities with practical motivation and variable (often factual) personality.

LOCOMOTIVE ENGINEER Spatial, technical aptitudes. Personality factual and tending towards passive. Motivation towards practical and research.

LORRY DRIVER see TRUCK DRIVER.

LOSS ADJUSTER see INSURANCE ADJUSTER.

MACHINIST Spatial aptitudes, a passive personality and creative/practical motivation.

MAINTENANCE TECHNICIAN Technical ability with an FLPI personality and practical motivation.

MAITRE D' Aptitudes vary, sometimes complex, whilst personality may be towards the excitable and aggressive. Some creative motivation may appear, though sometimes executive or social.

MAKE-UP ARTIST Variable abilities (often spatial) with a feeling, calm and independent personality and creative motivation.

MANAGEMENT CONSULTANT Above average verbal, complex and analytical abilities with a factual, calm and independent personality and executive motivation.

MANAGEMENT SERVICES ANALYST Above average analytical ability (often verbal and numerical strengths). Factual personality and practical and administrative motivation.

MANAGING DIRECTOR Usually above average abilities with particular strengths and numerical and verbal; FCAI personality with executive motivation.

MANUFACTURING ENGINEER Numerical, spatial or technical aptitudes, frequently complex and coding as well. Personality factual and independent. Motivation practical and research.

MANUFACTURING MANAGER Numerical, technical, complex aptitudes. A factual, calm, group and fairly aggressive personality. Motivation practical and social with perhaps some executive interest as well.

MARINE BIOLOGIST Well above average perceptual and analytical abilities; often independent personality with research motivation.

MARINE ENGINEER Technical aptitudes, also numerical and spatial for design level. Personality factual and with practical, research motivation.

MARKET GARDENER Variable abilities, but often spatial and technical strengths, with an independent and passive personality and practical motivation.

MARKET RESEARCHER Acuity and analytical abilities with a factual, calm and independent personality and research and administrative motivation.

MARKETING DIRECTOR/MANAGER Verbal, spatial and numerical skills, FLAI personality and executive motivation.

MASSEUR/MASSEUSE FLPG personality and social and practical motivation, but abilities are more variable.

MATERIALS HANDLER Technical aptitudes, a factual personality and practical motivation required.

MATERIALS SCIENTIST Above average ability (often perceptual and analytical supported by technical skills); research motivation but personality more variable (although often factual and independent).

MATHEMATICIAN Numerical and analytical skills and well above average ability, often factual and independent personality with research and administrative motivation.

MECHANIC Technical ability, often factual personality and practical motivation.

MECHANICAL ENGINEER Well above average numerical and technical abilities with practical motivation and variable personality, depending on working environment.

MEDICAL ILLUSTRATOR Perceptual and spatial abilities; factual, calm and frequently independent personality with creative and research motivation.

MEDICAL PHOTOGRAPHER Perceptual aptitudes, often spatial ones as well. Personality passive and usually independent. Motivation likely to combine creative and research.

MEDICAL PHYSICS TECHNICIAN Aptitudes need to be technical and/or spatial with coding as well. Personality is factual, calm, passive and independent. Motivation is strongly research oriented.

MEDICAL RECORDS OFFICER Perceptual and acuity abilities with social and administrative motivation but variable personality, depending on type of working environment.

MEDICAL REPRESENTATIVE Verbal and perceptual abilities; factual, independent and aggressive personality and executive and research motivation.

MEDICAL SECRETARY Perceptual and acuity abilities, social and administrative motivation but with more variable personality – although often calm and aggressive.

MENTAL NURSE Above average all round ability, ECPG personality and social motivation.

MERCHANDISER Spatial and acuity abilities; often factual, independent and aggressive personality with creative and administrative motivation.

MERCHANT SAILOR Variable abilities (often technical strengths) with a reasonably factual and group-orientated personality and practical motivation.

METALLURGIST Well above average technical and analytical abilities; factual (often independent) personality, research and practical motivation.

METEOROLOGIST Well above average ability, factual and often independent personality and research motivation.

MICROELECTRONICS ENGINEER Numerical, spatial and coding aptitudes appear at a high level. Personality is factual and generally calm. Personality is research and practical.

MIDWIFE Above average ability; calm, independent and moderately aggressive personality with social motivation.

MILITARY POLICE OFFICER Various aptitudes probably highest in technical, visual and sometimes complex areas. Personality is factual and aggressive, whilst motivation is practical.

MILKMAN Variable abilities (numerical skills help), CPI personality and practical and social motivation.

MILLER Variable abilities, but technical and acuity skills help. Often factual and independent personality with practical and research motivation.

MILLINER Spatial ability with variable personality and practical motivation.

MINER Variable abilities, calm and group-orientated personality, practical motivation.

MINING ENGINEER Spatial, technical and numerical aptitudes. Factual, calm and independent personality with research and practical motivation.

MINISTER OF RELIGION Verbal ability; factual, calm and independent personality and social and administrative motivation.

MODEL (FASHION/GRAPHIC) Variable abilities with ELPI personality.

MODEL MAKER Technical ability supported by spatial skills; ELAI personality with practical motivation.

MOTOR MECHANIC Technical aptitudes as well as a factual personality and practical motivation.

MOUNTED POLICE OFFICER Varied abilities, factual, independent personality and practical motivation.

MUSEUM ASSISTANT Variable abilities (often spatial and technical skills help at professional level) with a calm and passive personality and creative and research motivation.

MUSIC THERAPIST Above average ability with a feeling and lively personality and social and creative motivation.

MUSICIAN (ORCHESTRAL) Above average ability with an ELAI personality and creative motivation. Talent also helps!

NANNY Variable abilities; ECPI personality and social motivation.

NATURE CONSERVANCY WARDEN Variable abilities, with spatial and technical helpful; independent personality and practical motivation.

NATUROPATH Perceptual aptitudes are usually strong. Personality is feeling, passive and likely to be independent. Motivation may combine research with creative.

NAVAL ARCHITECT High numerical and spatial aptitudes with a factual personality as well as research motivation, perhaps with a creative interest as well are the most likely blend of talents for this career.

NAVIGATING OFFICER Spatial and acuity abilities, with factual, calm and independent personality and research and practical motivation.

NEGOTIATOR Variable abilities (numerical skills help); often aggressive and independent personality and executive motivation.

NEUROSURGEON High numerical, perceptual and complex aptitudes. A factual, calm personality and a research motivation.

NEWSPAPER REPORTER/PHOTOGRAPHER *see* REPORTER.

NOTARY PUBLIC Verbal, numerical and acuity abilities. Personality towards independent and calm. Administrative motivation sometimes with executive as well.

NOVELIST Verbal ability, strongly independent personality and literary motivation plus talent and luck!

NUCLEAR PHYSICIST Above average numerical and perceptual abilities, often factual, calm and independent personality; research and practical motivation.

NURSE Above average ability with an FCPG personality and social and research motivation.

NURSERY NURSE ECPG personality and social motivation.

NUTRITIONIST Above average perceptual and analytical abilities; factual and excitable personality and research and social motivation.

OBSTETRICIAN *see* DOCTOR.

OCCUPATIONAL HEALTH NURSE Perceptual aptitudes, a factual personality and research as well as social motivation.

OCCUPATIONAL PSYCHOLOGIST Well above average verbal and analytical abilities, usually factual and independent personality with social and research motivation.

OCCUPATIONAL THERAPIST Above average abilities (particularly technical and acuity skills); calm and independent personality with social and practical motivation.

OCEANOGRAPHER Numerical and coding aptitudes feature strongly as does an FCPI personality with research motivation.

OFFICE CLEANER Variable abilities, with an often independent and lively personality and practical motivation.

OFFICE MACHINERY MECHANIC Technical ability with an FLPI personality and practical and administrative motivation.

OFFICE MANAGER Numerical and acuity abilities; factual but not passive personality and administrative and executive motivation.

OIL RIG WORKER Technical ability; factual and independent personality and practical motivation.

OPERATIONAL RESEARCHER Well above average numerical ability with an FCPI personality and research and administrative motivation.

OPHTHALMIC OPTICIAN Above average ability (particularly in spatial and acuity areas); often factual and independent personality with research and social motivation.

OPTICIAN see DISPENSING OPTICIAN.

ORGANIZATION AND METHODS OFFICER see WORK STUDY OFFICER.

ORTHODONTIST see DENTIST.

ORTHOPTIST Above average technical ability with a calm (but not feeling) personality, social and research motivation.

OSTEOPATH Above average ability, an ECAG personality and social motivation.

OUTPLACEMENT CONSULTANT Verbal, analytical aptitudes and an aggressive, group personality with social and executive motivation.

PACKER Varied abilities. A passive personality and practical motivation.

PAINTER Spatial aptitudes will normally appear most strongly. An independent personality and creative motivation frequently appear.

PANEL BEATER Spatial and technical abilities, a variable personality, depending on working environment, and practical motivation.

PAPER MANUFACTURING WORKER Technical aptitudes are useful with a factual personality and practical motivation.

PARAMEDIC Various visual aptitudes can feature strongly. Personality tends to be passive and factual. Motivation is practical and can also be social.

PARCELFORCE STAFF Varied aptitudes with personality that tends to be passive with practical motivation.

PATENT AGENT Verbal and technical abilities (usually above average); with an FCPI personality and practical and literary motivation.

PATENT EXAMINER Above average technical and analytical abilities; factual, calm and independent personality with practical and research motivation.

PATHOLOGIST Well above average perceptual and analytic abilities (supported by acuity skills); factual, independent personality (often calm and aggressive) with research and practical motivation.

PATTERN CUTTER Spatial and technical abilities, often factual and passive personality with practical motivation.

PERSONAL TRAINER Perceptual aptitudes are often found together with an excitable, passive and group personality. Motivation is social and may also be practical.

PERSONNEL DIRECTOR Verbal ability and an ECAI personality with executive motivation.

PERSONNEL OFFICER Verbal and acuity abilities and social motivation. Personality is more variable, but often factual.

PHARMACIST Well above average perceptual and acuity abilities; factual, independent (often aggressive) personality and research and social motivation.

PHARMACOLOGIST Well above average perceptual and acuity abilities with a factual and independent personality and research motivation.

PHILOSOPHER Well above average verbal and analytical abilities and literary motivation. Personality more variable, but usually independent.

PHOTOGRAPHER Spatial abilities with an independent personality and creative and research motivation.

PHOTOGRAPHIC TECHNICIAN Technical and acuity abilities, often with a calm and independent personality and practical motivation.

PHYSICAL EDUCATION TEACHER Above average ability; usually factual, excitable personality and social and practical motivation.

PHYSICIST Well above average complex, numerical and technical abilities, factual personality (frequently independent), research and practical motivation.

PHYSIOTHERAPIST Above average ability with a calm, independent personality and social and practical motivation.

PIANO TUNER Acuity ability; often feeling and calm personality with practical motivation.

PICTURE FRAMER Spatial ability; often independent and passive personality and creative and practical motivation.

PILOT (AEROPLANE) Numerical, spatial, complex aptitudes. Factual, calm, independent characteristics emerge as well as practical, research and executive motivation.

PILOT (COASTAL) Usually technical aptitudes, may be spatial as well. Factual and calm personality with practical motivation.

PLANNING TECHNICIAN Spatial, numerical and acuity aptitudes. Personality tends to be passive, whilst motivation is a mixture of creative, practical and administrative.

PLASTERER Spatial ability with variable personality (often calm and independent) with practical motivation.

PLAY LEADER Variable abilities with an FLPG personality and social motivation.

PLUMBER Spatial and technical abilities; variable personality (often factual and independent) with practical motivation.

POET Verbal ability with a feeling and independent personality and literary motivation.

POLICE DOG HANDLER see POLICE OFFICER, but maybe less group oriented and less social motivation.

POLICE OFFICER Above average ability with an FCPG personality and social and practical motivation.

POLITICAL AGENT Variable abilities with an FLAG personality and executive motivation.

POLITICIAN Verbal ability, FLAG personality and executive motivation.

POOL AND SPA OPERATOR Technical aptitudes and a factual, passive, independent personality with practical motivation.

PORTER Varied aptitudes, a personality tending to be passive and often independent with practical motivation.

POSTMAN/WOMAN Variable abilities with a calm and independent personality, social and practical motivation.

POST OFFICE CLERK Numerical ability, often factual, passive and group-orientated personality with administrative motivation.

POTTER Spatial ability with an ECPI personality and creative and practical motivation.

PRIEST/CLERGYMAN see MINISTER OF RELIGION.

PRINCIPAL NURSING OFFICER Above average ability; ECAG personality, social and administrative motivation.

PRINTER Spatial and technical abilities with independent personality and a literary and practical motivation.

PRISON OFFICER Variable abilities with an FCPG personality and social and practical motivation.

PROBATION OFFICER Variable abilities with a factual personality and social motivation.

PROCESS WORKER (eg FOOD) see FOOD SERVICE WORKER.

PRODUCER (FILMS etc) Variable ability (numerical skills helpful); factual and independent personality (often aggressive), literary and executive motivation.

PRODUCTION MANAGER Above average technical and numerical abilities with an FCAG personality and executive and practical motivation.

PROGRAMMER see COMPUTER PROGRAMMER.

PROOF READER Above average verbal and acuity abilities with a passive and independent personality and literary motivation.

PROPERTY NEGOTIATOR Numerical and verbal abilities with an FLAI personality and executive motivation.

PROSTHETICS ENGINEER Technical and spatial aptitudes should be pronounced. A factual personality with motivation that is research oriented with some practical interest as well.

PSYCHIATRIC SOCIAL WORKER Variable abilities; factual, aggressive and group-orientated personality and social motivation.

PSYCHOANALYST Above average verbal ability with an ECPI personality and social motivation.

PSYCHOLOGIST Above average, complex, verbal and analytical abilities with an ELAI or ECAG personality and social motivation.

PSYCHOTHERAPIST Variable abilities (above average for professional qualifications); ECPG personality with literary and social motivation.

PUBLICAN Variable abilities (numerical skills help); FCAG personality and executive and practical motivation.

PUBLICITY AGENT Verbal and numerical abilities with an aggressive and group-orientated personality and executive motivation.

PUBLIC RELATIONS DIRECTOR/MANAGER Above average verbal ability with an ELAG personality and executive motivation.

PUBLIC RELATIONS EXECUTIVE Verbal ability with FLAG personality and literary and executive motivation.

PUBLISHER Verbal and spatial abilities with an FLAI personality and literary and executive motivation.

PURCHASING MANAGER Numerical aptitudes likely to be the highest, though may have strong perceptual aptitudes as well. Personality may be factual or feeling, calm or excitable depending upon the product or service, but otherwise is likely to be independent and aggressive. Executive motivation.

PURSER Above average numerical ability; independent and aggressive personality and administrative motivation. (This position increasingly requires professional accountancy qualifications.)

QUALITY CONTROLLERS Above average technical and analytical abilities with factual and independent personality and research and practical motivation.

QUALITY INSPECTORS Technical and acuity abilities, often independent personality and practical motivation.

QUANTITY SURVEYOR Well above average numerical and technical abilities with a factual, passive and independent personality and practical and administrative motivation.

RACEHORSE JOCKEY Varied abilities. Personality likely to be factual, aggressive and independent. Motivation is practical.

RACING CAR DRIVER Varied aptitudes, but likely to be high on spatial. Factual, aggressive personality and practical motivation, perhaps with some executive interest as well.

RADIOGRAPHER Above average ability with perceptual and spatial skills particularly useful; normally a calm and independent personality with scientific and research motivation.

RADIO PRESENTER see TELEVISION AND RADIO PRESENTER.

RAILWAY DRIVER Technical abilities useful as are spatial ones. FCPI personality and practical motivation.

RAILWAY GUARD Mixed abilities with a factual, calm and often independent personality and social and practical motivation.

RAILWAY TRACK WORKER Technical and spatial aptitudes should be strong. Factual personality with practical motivation.

RATING VALUATION OFFICER Above average ability (numerical specialization helpful); FCPI personality and practical and administrative motivation.

RECEPTIONIST Variable abilities (acuity, numerical and verbal strengths useful); variable personality according to employment environment, literary and administrative motivation.

RECORDING ENGINEER Numerical and spatial aptitudes likely to predominate. Personality may tend towards feeling and sometimes excitable. Motivation may be a mix of research and creative.

RECREATION CENTRE STAFF/MANAGER Acuity skills are valuable. Varied personality but tending to be more aggressive in management. Motivation may combine elements of social, administrative and executive.

REFLEXOLOGIST Perceptual aptitudes are likely to be strong. Personality is feeling, passive and independent. Motivation combines elements of creative, social and research.

REFUSE COLLECTOR No specific aptitudes, often factual personality with practical motivation.

REMEDIAL TEACHER Above average ability with an ECPG personality and social motivation.

RENOVATOR Spatial aptitudes are usually required. Varied personality types though generally calm. Motivation practical and creative.

REPORTER Above average ability, particularly verbal, with aggressive, independent personality and literary motivation.

RESORT REPRESENTATIVE Variable abilities. Excitable and aggressive personality and normally group oriented. Motivation may be a blend of creative, social, executive and practical.

RESTORER Variable abilities (spatial and technical skills help), often with a calm and independent personality and creative and research motivation.

RETAIL ASSISTANT see RETAIL MANAGER, though personality tends to be more passive.

RETAIL MANAGER Variable abilities (numerical skills useful); FCAG personality and social and executive motivation.

RIDING INSTRUCTOR see HORSE RIDING INSTRUCTOR.

ROAD TRANSPORT MANAGER Technical and acuity aptitudes. Factual and aggressive personality and practical as well as administrative motivation.

ROOFER Spatial and technical abilities, often with a calm, aggressive and independent personality and practical motivation.

ROUGHNECK Technical aptitudes, factual personality and practical motivation.

ROUSTABOUT Technical aptitudes, factual (sometimes aggressive personality if leading) and practical motivation.

SADDLER Spatial ability with a variable personality, depending on occupational environment, but often independent with practical motivation.

SAILOR (MERCHANT NAVY) see MERCHANT SAILOR.

SALES ASSISTANT see RETAIL ASSISTANT.

SALES EXECUTIVE Verbal ability with an excitable but not passive personality and executive and administrative motivation.

SALES MANAGER Verbal (and often numerical) abilities with an FLAG personality and executive motivation.

SALESPERSON Verbal ability with group-orientated personality and social and executive motivation.

SALES TRAINER Variable abilities (often verbal strengths) with a factual and often aggressive personality and social motivation.

SCAFFOLDER Technical aptitudes, though spatial are useful to have as well. Factual personality and practical motivation.

SCIENCE TEACHER Above average ability (particularly in perceptual and verbal areas) with a calm and factual personality and social and research motivation.

SCIENCE WRITER Verbal and perceptual abilities with a factual and independent personality and literary and research motivation.

SCIENTIFIC INSTRUMENT MAKER Perceptual and technical abilities with an FCPI personality and research and practical motivation.

SCRIPTWRITER see WRITER.

SCULPTOR Spatial ability, and ELAI personality. Creative and practical motivation, and talent!

SECRETARY/PA Verbal and acuity abilities with literary and administrative motivation. Personality is more variable, depending on work environment, but will often be calm and moderately independent.

SECURITIES ANALYST Above average analytical and numerical abilities with a factual and independent personality and administrative motivation.

SECURITY OFFICER Variable abilities with a factual, calm and independent personality. Practical and administrative motivation.

SERVICE ENGINEER/TECHNICIAN Technical aptitudes, a factual, independent personality and practical motivation.

SESSION MUSICIAN Variable abilities with an ECAI personality and creative motivation; plus talent and luck!

SET DESIGNER Spatial and technical abilities, often with a feeling and independent personality and creative motivation.

SEWING MACHINIST Variable abilities; often passive and group-orientated personality and practical motivation.

SHELF FILLER Variable abilities and personality with practical motivation.

SHEPHERD Variable abilities; ECPI personality and practical motivation together with a love of the outdoor life.

SHIPPING AND FORWARDING OFFICER Verbal and numerical abilities with administrative motivation. Personality more variable, depending on occupational environment.

SHIPPING PILOT Numerical and spatial abilities often with excellent acuity skills. Often calm and independent personality and practical motivation.

SHOP ASSISTANT Variable abilities (numerical and acuity skills useful); ELPI personality and executive motivation.

SHOP FITTER Spatial and acuity abilities; variable personality, but often feeling and independent with creative and practical motivation.

SIGN WRITER Verbal, spatial and acuity abilities; often a feeling, calm and independent personality with creative and practical motivation.

SILVERSMITH Spatial and technical abilities; feeling, passive and independent personality with creative and some practical motivation.

SINGER see MUSICIAN.

SOCIAL SCIENTIST Above average ability with an ECAI personality and social and research motivation.

SOCIAL WORKER Above average abilities with an ECAG personality and social and administrative motivation.

SOFTWARE ENGINEER Numerical, spatial and coding aptitude. Factual, independent personality. Research motivation usually strongest.

SOLDIER Variable abilities (increasingly technical skills required) with an FCPG personality and social and practical motivation.

SOLICITOR Well above average verbal ability, FCAI personality and literary and administrative motivation.

SOUND ENGINEER Above average technical and numerical abilities with variable personality, but often aggressive and independent. Creative and practical motivation.

SPACE SALESPERSON Numerical, analytical, spatial aptitudes likely to be strong. Personality tends to be factual, aggressive and independent. Motivation likely to be executive and creative, sometimes administrative.

SPEECH AND DRAMA TEACHER Above average verbal abilities. Feeling and aggressive personality and social and literary motivation.

SPEECH THERAPIST Well above average ability. Feeling, independent and often excitable personality with literary and social motivation.

SPORTS CENTRE MANAGER Numerical and acuity skills. Aggressive personality with executive and/or social motivation.

SPORTS COACH Variable abilities and often an excitable, aggressive personality with social and practical motivation.

SPORTS OFFICIAL (REFEREE) see SPORTS COACH.

STABLEHAND see GROOM.

STAGE DESIGNER see SET DESIGNER.

STAGE HAND Variable abilities; calm personality (often slightly aggressive and group biased) with creative and practical motivation.

STAGE MANAGER Variable abilities (increasingly technical strengths); calm, aggressive and independent personality with a literary and practical motivation.

STATISTICIAN Well above average numerical abilities (acuity skills needed for a statistics producer and analytical for an analyst). Factual and independent personality with research and administrative motivation.

STEWARD see AIR CABIN CREW. Also for careers for stewards at sea.

STOCK CONTROLLER Numerical and acuity abilities with a variable personality, depending upon employment environment, but often factual, passive and independent, with practical and administrative motivation.

STOCKBROKER Numerical aptitudes, sometimes complex as well. Aggressive, independent personality and executive motivation.

STONE MASON Spatial abilities with an often independent, feeling personality and creative motivation.

STOREKEEPER see STOCK CONTROLLER.

STUDIO ASSISTANT Variable abilities (often technical skills needed); passive and independent personality (often excitable) with creative and social motivation.

STUNT PERFORMER Technical aptitudes predominate. An aggressive, independent and factual personality with practical motivation.

SURGEON Well above average ability (particularly in complex, perceptual and analytical areas); calm, independent personality with research motivation.

SURVEYOR Numerical and spatial abilities with factual and calm personality (often independent) and research and practical motivation.

SYSTEMS ADMINISTRATOR see database administrator. In dealing with systems, can be more involved with network and services.

SYSTEMS ANALYST Well above average numerical and analytical abilities; FCPI personality and research and administrative motivation.

TAILOR Spatial abilities with a variable personality, depending on occupational environment, and practical motivation.

TAX INSPECTOR/ADVISER Above average numerical abilities; factual, independent (often aggressive) personality with executive and administrative motivation.

TAXI DRIVER Variable abilities; an excitable and often aggressive personality (but not strongly group-orientated) with social and practical motivation.

TAXIDERMIST Variable abilities (often spatial and technical strengths); calm and independent personality with practical motivation.

TEACHER Above average ability (often verbal strengths) with an ECAG personality and social motivation.

TEACHER OF FINE ART AND CRAFTS Similar to teacher, but with higher spatial ability and social and creative motivation.

TEACHER OF HANDICAPPED Similar to teacher, but with less emphasis on verbal skills.

TECHNICAL REPRESENTATIVE Verbal and technical abilities with factual, independent and sometimes aggressive personality and executive and research motivation.

TECHNICAL WRITER Above average verbal and technical abilities. Independent, calm and often passive personality and literary and practical or research motivation.

TELECOMMUNICATIONS ENGINEER Numerical and technical abilities. Factual personality, often excitable and group-orientated with practical motivation.

TELEPHONE CALL CENTRE STAFF Varied aptitudes and personality, often with executive or administrative motivation.

TELEPHONIST Variable abilities but acuity skills useful; excitable, group-orientated personality most predominant with social and practical motivation.

TELEVISION ENGINEER Numerical and technical abilities (usually above average) with a factual and independent often aggressive personality and practical motivation.

TELEVISION PRODUCTION ASSISTANT Variable ability but acuity skills useful, with a calm and independent personality and creative and literary motivation.

TELEVISION or RADIO PRESENTER Verbal ability with an excitable, independent personality and creative and executive motivation.

TEXTILE DESIGNER Spatial aptitudes need to be very good. Personality mainly feeling and passive, whilst motivation is creative.

THATCHER Spatial ability with an ECPI personality and practical motivation.

THEATRE ADMINISTRATOR Above average verbal and numerical abilities; calm and independent personality with creative and administrative motivation.

THEATRE COSTUME DESIGNER see TEXTILE DESIGNER.

TILER Spatial and acuity abilities with a calm (often independent) personality and practical motivation.

TOOL MAKER Technical and numerical abilities, factual and independent personality and practical motivation.

TOURISM INFORMATION OFFICER Acuity skills an advantage. Personality likely to be passive. Motivation may be a blend of social, practical, creative and administrative.

TOWN PLANNING OFFICER Verbal, numerical, perceptual, acuity and coding abilities. A calm and passive personality together with administrative motivation.

TOY MAKER Technical and spatial abilities with practical motivation. Personality more variable according to employment environment.

TRACER Spatial and acuity abilities; FLAI personality and practical and administrative motivation.

TRADER Variable abilities (numerical skills useful) with a factual and excitable personality and practical motivation.

TRADING STANDARDS OFFICER Acuity and coding skills are important. Factual, calm and independent personality. Motivation is mainly administrative, but may also include research and practical.

TRAFFIC WARDEN Variable abilities; factual and independent personality. Practical and administrative motivation.

TRAIN DRIVER Variable abilities; calm and independent personality and practical motivation.

TRAINING OFFICER Above average general ability; ECAI personality and social and practical motivation.

TRANSLATOR Verbal and acuity abilities; variable personality (but often feeling, calm and independent), literary and administrative motivation.

TRANSPORT MANAGER Variable abilities, an FCAG personality and executive and practical motivation.

TRAVEL AGENT Verbal and numerical abilities with often a factual, excitable and moderately independent personality and executive and administrative motivation.

TRAVEL COURIER see RESORT REPRESENTATIVE.

TRUCK DRIVER Variable abilities with an FCPI personality and practical motivation.

TURF ACCOUNTANT Above average numerical ability with an FLPI personality and executive and administrative motivation.

TV CAMERA OPERATOR *see* FILM CAMERA OPERATOR.

TYPIST Acuity skills are predominant but verbal ability is useful; variable personality depending on employment environment, and administrative motivation.

TYRE/EXHAUST FITTER Technical aptitudes, factual personality and practical motivation.

UMPIRE Variable aptitudes but a calm personality and usually with social and/or practical motivation.

UNDERTAKER *see* FUNERAL DIRECTOR.

UNDERWRITER Above average numerical abilities. Independent and factual personality. Administrative and executive motivation.

UNION NEGOTIATOR Variable abilities with an ELAG personality and executive motivation.

UPHOLSTERER Spatial ability with an often calm and independent personality and practical motivation.

URBAN PLANNER *see* TOWN PLANNING OFFICER.

VAN DRIVER Variable aptitudes and personality. Practical motivation.

VEHICLE BODY BUILDER Spatial as well as technical aptitudes. Factual, independent personality. Practical and sometimes creative motivation.

VETERINARY NURSE Variable abilities. Feeling and usually calm and independent personality and practical motivation.

VETERINARY SURGEON Well above average ability; independent and moderately feeling personality with executive and research motivation.

VISION MIXER Above average spatial and technical abilities; calm personality and creative motivation.

VOCATIONAL COUNSELLOR *see* CAREERS ADVISER.

WAGES CLERK Numerical and acuity skills. Factual, passive personality with administrative motivation.

WAITER/WAITRESS Variable abilities; ELPI personality and social and practical motivation.

WARDEN (COUNTRYSIDE/TRAFFIC) Independent personality and practical motivation.

WATCH AND CLOCK REPAIRER Spatial and technical abilities; often calm and independent personality and practical motivation.

WATER ENGINEER Spatial, technical, numerical aptitudes. Factual personality with practical and research motivation.

WEATHER FORECASTER Numerical and spatial aptitudes, possibly also verbal aptitude. Factual, calm, passive personality. Motivation tending towards research.

WEB DESIGNER Numerical, complex, spatial aptitudes. Personality tending towards feeling and independent, motivation creative and research.

WEB MASTER (content, development and technical) Analytical, coding, numerical aptitudes. Personality passive and independent, motivation a mixture of research, creative and literary.

WEB PRODUCER Not normally technical like web masters. Verbal aptitudes, more assertive. Motivation towards literary, executive and administrative.

WEIR KEEPER see LOCK KEEPER.

WELDER Spatial aptitudes, factual, calm personality and practical motivation.

WINDOW CLEANER Independent personality and practical motivation.

WINDOW DRESSER Spatial ability, feeling (often excitable and independent) personality and creative motivation.

WORD PROCESSOR OPERATOR Verbal and acuity abilities, variable personality according to employment environment but often factual and passive, with administrative motivation.

WORK STUDY OFFICER Above average ability with an FCAI personality and research and practical motivation.

WRITER Verbal ability, independent personality and literary motivation.

YOUTH WORKER Variable ability, ECAG personality and social (often practical) motivation.

ZOO KEEPER Variable ability with calm and independent personality and practical motivation.

ZOOLOGIST Well above average perceptual (and often numerical) abilities, usually with a calm, independent and passive personality and research motivation.